Gleacton

Books, Lessons, Ideas

for Teaching the Six Traits

**Writing at Middle
and High School**

election

Books, Lessons, Ideas

for Teaching the Six Traits

Writing at Middle and High School

Compiled and Annotated by Vicki Spandel, Write Traits

Great Source Education Group

Wilmington, MA

Great Source® is a registered trademark of Houghton Mifflin Company.

Printed in the United States of America

International Standard Book Number: 0-669-48175-0

4 5 6 7 8 9 10 - MP - 05 04 03

Table of Contents

Introduction

Welcome! We're pleased to present our year 2000 bibliography written especially for teachers who work with the six traits in their classrooms. This bibliography is divided into seven sections: one for each of the six traits and a last section of resources for you.

How books are listed. Books to use in teaching the six traits to students are listed alphabetically, but in addition are grouped by trait: books to use when teaching ideas, books to use when teaching organization, and so on. We hope this will make it very easy for you to find just what you are looking for. Remember, though, just because you use a book to teach *ideas* is no reason you could not also use it to teach *voice* or *fluency*—or any trait. We've simply identified books that have particular strengths in particular traits. Each reference is annotated and recommended grade levels are noted. In addition, all books for the six traits include suggested lesson plans connected to writing. They are *only* suggestions; you may have your own lessons in mind.

The Teacher Resource section at the end also lists books alphabetically by author. These titles, too, are annotated to help you choose the ones that appeal to you.

Last but not least, we're introducing "Vic's Picks" with this edition, a handy, new feature that lists must-have titles that no writing teacher should be without when modeling each trait for kids. Whether you're crunched for time in planning a lesson or need an on-the-spot selection, we hope you can use "Vic's Picks" to help zero in on titles that set the standard. Just look for the graphic icon flagging the title.

A wide range of resources. We have made a concerted effort to include books that appeal to students of many ages, interests, and abilities. Accordingly, you will find everything from poetry to technical writing, including books to entice middle schoolers and books to challenge high school writers.

We expect this collection to grow in both size and diversity in future editions. So, if your favorite book is not included yet, perhaps you'll see it next time around. It is *never* possible to put in everything; there is *always* another book to be discovered! We know we have not found them all and we *are* still hunting. We can tell you this, though; every book here has been carefully hand-selected for inclusion because it's a book we believe will help you enrich your writing curriculum and help students make strong connections between literature and writing.

How to use the bibliography. We suggest you take it trait by trait. As you teach a trait, skim through the selections to see which books might suit your grade level or teaching style or curriculum. Do not feel compelled to use all our recommendations, of course. Mix our suggestions with your own tried and true favorites.

Don't take us too literally! We have indicated for each student selection the grade levels we felt were most suitable, but feel free to disagree and to take liberties. As every good teacher of reading or writing knows, high schoolers are often fascinated and amused by picture books we might not think to share because they seem too "unsophisticated"; but often, a picture book makes just the point you wish to make and does it in both a concise and entertaining fashion. Just as frequently, younger reader/writers surprise us with the insight and interest they bring to a text we might have too hastily dismissed as over their heads. In short, rely on your own good judgment and knowledge of your students, using our categories as indicators, not rigid parameters. By the way, we are using *middle school* for grades 6–8 and *high school* for grades 9–12. (Some books designated as appropriate for middle or high school are so identified *not* because of reading level but because they provide a good starting point for more sophisticated discussion or writing activities.)

What about reading just for the fun of it? DO read aloud to your students for the pure joy of it. Though we've included *many* lesson ideas—and hope they'll spark your imagination and help you come up with even more—the truth is that you enhance students' lives and learning just by sharing books aloud. Students love being read to. Don't most of us? When you read to them, you share the message that reading is a pleasure and that you love good writing.

Besides, you *are* teaching the six traits *just by reading examples* of fine detail, strategic organization (great leads and conclusions), powerful voice, precise word choice, and lyrical fluency. So even if your primary purpose is to reinforce students' understanding of the traits, it is not necessary to follow up *each* book with a writing lesson. That part is always optional.

Pick and choose. Remember too that you do not need to read *an entire book* to make a point about detail or voice or whatever. Bits and pieces can be magical—and sufficient. Besides, a short passage only takes moments to share. One unforgettable phrase, rousing conclusion, engaging lead, or fluent line makes for a quick lesson in fine writing. You will probably read entire picture books, but with a longer selection, such as *How the Irish Saved Civilization,* you may read just a page or two—or even a single paragraph. You accomplish two things by this: You make your point about voice or detail, and you invite students who loved the selection to read more on their own.

Are these the books we see at Write Traits conferences? Yes. These are the very same books we display at our workshops and conferences. Of course, you'll *always* find new additions popping up in our displays because we love books and can't resist making our collection grow. We'll try to capture those new additions in future publications.

Books
for Teaching
Ideas

Ideas are all about information. Two things make ideas work well: clarity and detail. The books within this section have been selected because they present information very clearly, make technical or difficult-to-grasp ideas reader friendly, or make use of unusual or unexpected detail that goes well beyond the routine. Many of the selections feature striking imagery or language that appeals to the senses. Each book can help show students the importance of presenting information clearly and completely in order to make writing appealing and understandable for a specific audience.

Teach ideas by

- Reading aloud samples with good detail, good imagery
- Looking for details
- Filling in missing details
- Identifying "filler" (excess information)
- Comparing clarity in two or more passages

Anderson, Maggie and David Hassler, editors. *Learning By Heart: Contemporary American Poetry About School.* **1999. Iowa City: University of Iowa Press. ISBN: 0-87745-663-1.**

POETRY (MIDDLE SCHOOL, HIGH SCHOOL)

SUMMARY: See school through the eyes of America's finest contemporary poets. What a collection! You will dance your way through, finding many a passage to share aloud. What exactly do people learn about in school besides the usual menu of reading, math, writing, and geography? What about fear, depression, tension, love, joy, dreams, nostalgia, disappointment, and embarrassment? Perhaps success, too, if they are lucky. You and your students will hear many of your own feelings echoed in these lines.

LESSON IDEA: Read a number of poems aloud over a period of, say, two weeks or so. Then, create collages (3–5 poems per collage) of poems that speak to you or to your students. (Students can help make the choices, if you wish.) Give one collage to each group of 3–4 students (it is not necessary for each group to receive the same poems). Ask students to read and mark the poems, underlining favorite passages, posing questions, etc. Then, they can respond in any of several ways:

- Write a letter to one poet, asking questions or commenting on the poem
- Write a "response poem" dedicated to the poet; send it, if you wish
- Do, as a group, an interpretive reading of at least two of the poems— may be done choral reading style, with multiple voices, and students taking turns reading
- Write one poem each, expressing personal feelings or thoughts about school, and (as students are willing), share the group's personal collection aloud

Baker, Jeannie. *Window.* **1991. New York: HarperCollins Publishers. ISBN: 0-688-08917-8.**

PICTURE BOOK (PRIMARY THROUGH HIGH SCHOOL)

SUMMARY: Illustrated with amazing collage constructions, *Window* is a wordless picture book that tells a rich story of how events unfold and surroundings evolve. The pictures chronicle the changes in a young boy's life and in his environment, from babyhood to adulthood, all seen through the window of his room. Each picture is alive with details, but they're never the same, picture to picture. Use this book to help students become keen observers as they identify what has changed from one picture to another.

LESSON IDEA: After students have noticed the changes from picture to picture within the book, ask them to look out a window from their home and list what they see. With younger students, everyone can look out the school window as the teacher records observations. Wait two weeks, then follow up with the same activity, again including as many details as possible. Compare the lists to see what has changed. (You can continue this portion of the activity indefinitely.) Here's another way to use the lists of details: Ask each student, using one or both lists, to create a descriptive piece of writing. Younger students can use pictures to do all or part of their description. Older students who have made individual lists can try exchanging them to see if each can draw a picture to match the details listed by his/her partner. If the drawing is difficult to do, perhaps more details are needed! Note: If you continue the drawings over a period of time, you'll create your own picture books much like *Window.*

 Bartoletti, Susan Campbell. *Growing Up in Coal Country.* **1996. New York: Houghton Mifflin.** ISBN: **0-395-77847-6.**

VIC'S PICKS NONFICTION/HISTORICAL CHAPTER BOOK (MIDDLE SCHOOL, HIGH SCHOOL)

SUMMARY: The picture on the cover tells much of the story. Take time to look at those faces. It's so fascinating, you may choose to read the whole thing aloud, or you may choose selected excerpts. Either way, be sure to share the photographs within. They create atmosphere and mood.

LESSON IDEA: This book is an excellent example of how text, including nonfiction, is expanded through the use of photographs and quotations. You might use it for a lesson on just that. As you read the book, talk about the vivid images and the graphic details that help us understand what it was like to be a child or teenager working in coal mines. Talk about the quotations, too; isn't this one effective way to bring voice into nonfiction without compromising objectivity? Perhaps your students can find someone to interview who held a very different kind of job, say, thirty or more years ago. What are the salient details of that experience? Ask students to record them in a brief report, but to include at least two quotations that add spark. If they can also include a photograph or sketch, so much the better! **Alternative:** How would these young coal miners feel today if they could be alive and read this book? Ask students to do a book review from a miner's point of view: Did the writer capture the experience?

Baylor, Byrd. *I'm in Charge of Celebrations*. Illustrated by Peter Parnall. 1986. New York: Aladdin Paperbacks. ISBN: 0-689-80620-5.

Ideas 12

PICTURE BOOK (PRIMARY THROUGH MIDDLE SCHOOL)

SUMMARY: Little topics make the best topics. In this delightful, poetic book, the speaker finds magic in the world all around her; she celebrates dust devils, triple rainbows, green clouds, the sighting of a coyote, the flight of doves, lightning, and falling stars. Each is personal and important *just* to her. This is a fine book for showing students the value of personal topics.

LESSON IDEA: First, read the book. Then ask, what do you celebrate in your life? Forget national, legal holidays. Focus on celebrations based on personally important events (e.g., first cake I baked myself, the time I saw a falling star, finding a four-leaf clover, saving a stray cat). Write them up, then assemble a class book of the results: *We're in Charge of Celebrations.*

Bragg, Rick. *All Over But the Shoutin'*. 1997. New York: Pantheon. ISBN: 0-679-44258-8.

NONFICTION/HISTORICAL MEMOIR (HIGH SCHOOL)

SUMMARY: Gritty and realistic, Bragg's book is filled with images you cannot forget: e.g., "the wallpaper hung like dead skin . . ." (p. 53). It's a great read-aloud book, but since the whole thing runs more than 300 pages, you may wish to be selective about the passages you choose, allowing interested students to read the whole piece independently. Bragg's story of going from abject poverty to winning the Pulitzer Prize is remarkable enough, but he tells it in language so vibrant, you'll find yourself re-reading passages just for the joy of it. Excellent for word choice, too.

LESSON IDEA: Ask students to recall a time when the weather was almost unbearably hot. Then invite them, as a class, or in small groups or pairs, to brainstorm some words or phrases to describe the experience. Now, ask each pair or group of students to first write a 3–5 sentence mundane description of a hot day. Make it boring! For example, "It was hot. It was very hot. It was so hot you couldn't believe it . . ." etc. Finally, ask them to write a second short piece, only this time filling it with details to snag a reader's attention—referring to their original brainstormed lists. Now, ask groups to read their selections aloud, first the mundane, then the detailed. Talk about how detail influences not only ideas but also voice. Finally, share Rick Bragg's description from the beginning of Chapter 11, "Under a Hateful Sky"—just two paragraphs, the first one running only a single sentence. **Extension:** Using Rick Bragg's example from page 100, talk about the power of a single-sentence paragraph. Obviously, this is a writer's trick you would not want to overuse. When does it have power? When might it look more like an oversight? Why does Bragg use it here? Do you think it works?

Butler, Octavia. *Kindred.* **1988. Boston: Beacon Press.** ISBN: **0-8070-8305-4.**

HISTORICAL FICTION/SCIENCE FICTION (HIGH SCHOOL)

SUMMARY: An innovative, highly provocative book—also excellent for organization and for voice because of its rich language and unusual structure. Imagine a modern African American woman transported somehow into the world of the antebellum South, to a plantation where nothing is familiar. This is what happens not just once, but repeatedly to Dana, who time travels back and forth between these two worlds, raising as she does the haunting questions of morality and racial equality with which we live still. It's a page-turning story, full of adventure, brutality, mystery, and self-reflection—all the while exploring social issues in great depth and with much sensitivity. Captivating. Students need not be science fiction fans to enjoy this one.

LESSON IDEA: This book suggests two excellent ideas for writing exploration. First, students might transport themselves to another time in history, imagining how different their lives would be, what they would learn, and what lessons they would bring back with them to the twenty-first century. Alternatively, they might take a literary character from another time and bring him/her into the modern world. What observations would this person make? What lessons would he/she have to teach us? What important information from the "future" [our present] would he/she take back?

Cahill, Thomas. *How the Irish Saved Civilization.* **1996. New York: Doubleday.** ISBN: **0-385-41849-3.**

VIC'S PICKS

HISTORICAL NONFICTION CHAPTER BOOK (HIGH SCHOOL)

SUMMARY: Elegant, scholarly, and poetic all at once. Fasten your seatbelt because history was *never* like this. The language is not always easy, but its clarity comes from precision of use. Use this book to illustrate the power of vivid detail. In one early passage, Cahill brilliantly portrays the contrast between the Roman legions, almost languid in their confidence that they can never be overtaken or even threatened—they're *that* good—and the barbarians: chaotic, unkempt, ugly, wholly ignorant of what they're up against, and ignorant too (temporarily) of their own power.

LESSON IDEA: Read pages 14–15 and admire Cahill's sharp contrasts. Notice how the word "spiffy" jumps out at you. Ask students which images linger in their minds . . . anybody picturing carrots?

Ideas
14

Cleary, Beverly. *A Girl From Yamhill: A Memoir.* **1988. New York: William Morrow and Company, Inc.** ISBN: **0-688-07800-1.**

MEMOIR (ELEMENTARY THROUGH HIGH SCHOOL)

SUMMARY: If memoir interests you, this one is difficult to beat. Beverly Cleary has a knack for noticing everything in her world, and we're treated to her sharp-eyed vision on every page. This book vibrates with detail from the traditional Miss Falb (pronounced Fob) telling a confused Beverly to hold the pencil in her right hand (why was one hand wrong?) to Beverly's first kiss in fifth grade, an elegant brush on the fingers that left her breathless and blushing. The book is full of fascinating pictures from the good old days (Beverly grew up in the 1920s), but they aren't really needed. Cleary's words paint pictures that outshine the camera's efforts.

LESSON IDEA: Read a selected chapter aloud. Then invite students to share their own memoirs orally first, and then write them down. Oral storytelling, a great tradition in its own right, often jogs memories and builds confidence, not to mention encouraging detail from an engaged audience that may pose questions. Groups of three or four are ideal for this storytelling to writing transition. Any topic will do, but because students spend so much of their lives in school, school-related stories often come to mind more readily than some. Cleary shares many in her book that make for excellent starting points. Do not forget to share one of your own school experiences.

Collard, Sneed B. III. *Acting for Nature: What Young People Around the World Are Doing to Protect the Environment.* **1999. Berkeley, CA: Heyday Books.** ISBN: **1-890771-24-4.**

BIOGRAPHICAL ESSAYS (MIDDLE SCHOOL, HIGH SCHOOL)

SUMMARY: Ever wish *you* could be the one to rescue a sea turtle? You'll find inspiration in this most unusual book, a collection of true stories about what young people around the world have done to protect the environment. It's a roll up the sleeves look at how one individual truly can make a difference—from rescuing penguins off New Zealand to getting rid of trash in Durango, Colorado. Students will warm to the stories of other young people who have taken positive steps to make the world around them safer, cleaner, and more hospitable to plant and animal life. A book that encourages both action and a deep respect for the Earth.

LESSON IDEA: This makes an excellent read-aloud resource since every true-life story is an adventure, but you do not need to read every story; select a few and let students read others on their own. Follow up by writing to local environmental agencies for information or advice on what you might do to help protect your local environment. Students will gain excellent practice writing business letters, and will learn about problems or achievements in local environmental protection. Some students may wish to go a step further and participate in a local project to encourage exercise, build a new bike path, clean up a polluted stream or pond, or even help protect a threatened species through community awareness. Writing opportunities include not only reports, but posters, brochures, memos, letters, or even video scripts.

Ideas
15

Collard, Sneed B. III. *Alien Invaders: The Continuing Threat of Exotic Species.* **1996. Danbury, CT: Franklin Watts.** ISBN: **0-531-11298-5.**

NONFICTION SCIENCE ESSAYS (MIDDLE SCHOOL, HIGH SCHOOL)

SUMMARY: "Alien invaders" are species of any kind, from insects to plants and animals or viruses and bacteria, that have wandered far from their native homes, sometimes with disastrous (though never boring) results. Fire ants, so-named for their painful stings, originated in South America, for example, but have been sighted recently in Mobile, Alabama. They got there by hitchhiking on small imported plants. More than 4,500 alien species have "relocated" in the U.S. alone. Discover their fascinating, sometimes disturbing, stories in this extraordinarily well-written, brilliantly presented book. By the way, do NOT overlook the word choice in this ever-surprising account. You may wish to have students create a word list or even develop a dictionary for the book. Unusually lively language for an informational piece. (What impact does this have on voice?)

LESSON IDEA: This book suggests many possibilities. Following are just a few: Ask students to do a review of the book. How thorough and understandable is the information? Will it keep readers reading? As a related task, you might ask students to do a brief survey of the many ways information is presented in this book: notice indices, glossary, photographs, sidebars, graphs and charts, definitions, lists of sources . . . did we miss some? What does this tell us about the effective presentation of information in the twenty-first century? A third suggestion (you will need three or four copies of the book for this one): Because information is so easy to look up in this book, you might ask students, in groups, to devise simple quizzes—just two or three questions per group—then exchange to see if they can locate the answers their classmates have sent them in search of. Finally, compare this book to any science textbook or encyclopedia article: Which presents information more effectively? Why?

Collard, Sneed B. III. *Creepy Creatures.* **Illustrated by Kristin Kest. 1997. Watertown, MA: Charlesbridge Publishing.** ISBN: **0-88106-837-3.**

INFORMATIONAL CHAPTER BOOK/PICTURE BOOK (PRIMARY THROUGH HIGH SCHOOL)

SUMMARY: Excellently researched and ideal for teaching the importance of choosing the vivid, the little known, the startling detail. Use it with all ages. The entries are short, so you can share them quickly, and they contain a surprising amount of entertaining, striking information packed into a few words. Collard writes well, and knows what information to choose in the first place.

LESSON IDEA: Read several pieces aloud, pass out hard copy, or put them on the overhead: your choice. Then, after sharing, ask students to help identify the key details that make the piece work. What did you learn that was new or striking? Move from this to an encyclopedia entry, article from the Internet, or any informational piece to see if students, in pairs or groups, can successfully extract the same kinds of intriguing details. Then, have them write a short summary, using just that information—no filler! Share results aloud and talk about the importance of good research to good writing.

Collard, Sneed B. III. *Monteverde: Science and Scientists in a Costa Rican Cloud Forest.* **1997. Danbury, CT: Franklin Watts.** ISBN: **0-531-15901-9.**

SCIENCE CHAPTER BOOK (MIDDLE SCHOOL, HIGH SCHOOL)

SUMMARY: If ever there were a book to illustrate how to do informational writing well, this is it. Sneed combines photographs (many in glorious color), anecdotes, fact-filled exposition, quotations, bits of narrative, and biographical sketches to weave an informational piece that truly teaches and entertains us, too. As different from the encyclopedia approach as fresh-picked garden salad from yesterday's broccoli.

LESSON IDEA: Read the book yourself before deciding which passages to share with students (unless, of course, you decide to use it as a text, which you could certainly do). Choose a variety of pieces, some straightforward exposition, some anecdotal asides. Share the pictures, too. To bring closure, ask students to think about what makes good informational writing; most will conclude that a combination of writing styles and formats is important. Brainstorm a list of criteria you might use as a class to judge the quality of informational writing: e.g., completeness, accuracy, educational value to the reader, selection of intriguing details, and so on. Then, ask each student to identify <u>one</u> piece of informational writing—from a textbook, newspaper, the Internet, or wherever—to assess. Ask students also to write short paragraphs defending their assessments. Post the samples and the assessments so you can discuss what you have learned. Next time you do informational writing in your class, use the criteria you have created as a writing community to judge the quality of the writing *they* produce.

Cooper, Michael L. *Indian School: Teaching the White Man's Way.* 1999. Boston: Houghton Mifflin. ISBN: 0-395-92084-1.

HISTORICAL CHAPTER BOOK (MIDDLE SCHOOL, HIGH SCHOOL)

SUMMARY: Cooper's book presents a concise history of eighty-four Sioux boys and girls who were uprooted from their culture and transported, body and soul, to the Carlisle Indian School and the world of the whites. The pictures alone will haunt you. Their story is fascinating, disturbing, and inspiring, all at once. Some would not let their spirits die; for others, it was a tragic journey. Here is a portrait of supreme insensitivity—often promoted in the name of bettering Native American children's lives. This story has a semi-happy ending: Due to supreme efforts of many Native Americans and some whites as well, many whites began to value Native American culture and to encourage its emphasis in BIA schools.

LESSON IDEA: Talk first about Cooper's honesty, and about how he uses little details (many children did not know which way to put their pants on or why their hair had been cut) to make their everyday lives seem real to us. It is difficult to imagine being uprooted from your culture—but a fascinating idea for students to explore. Some may have experienced this firsthand—perhaps not under such rigid conditions as those imposed at the Carlisle School. Yet they may know how it feels to be in a culture where everything from language to hairstyles, music, dress, food, and religion is totally different. Ask students to reflect on this experience or to imagine a situation in which they are inserted into a new culture. How would it feel? What would be expected? Would they fight? Survive? Or give up? Might they embrace the new culture—or would they more likely reject it? Infinite answers are possible, and can make for some lively and imaginative writing.

Crutcher, Chris. *Ironman.* 1995. New York: William Morrow & Company, Inc. ISBN: 0-688-13503-X.

YOUNG ADULT NOVEL (MIDDLE SCHOOL, HIGH SCHOOL)

SUMMARY: Bo is a most unusual hero, one who dares think and live for himself, even when the personal stakes are high. Angry outbursts cause him to be assigned to an anger management group with the unforgettable Mr. Nak. Really, though, it is writing regularly to celebrity interviewer Larry King that keeps Bo sane. This is an excellent book for teaching organization because it alternates between the events of Bo's life and what's going on inside his head, which we learn through the letters. Use it in that way if you wish, perhaps inviting students to imitate this highly original organizational pattern. It works. The book is frank and charged with voice; both anger and adolescent angst come through loud and clear. (You may wish to preview it; the parent-child conflict is honest and sometimes disturbing.) Through it all though, Bo retains his fighting spirit.

LESSON IDEA: The organizational structure is one feature you will wish to point out to students. Here's another idea. Because this book brims with tension, it causes readers to think through moral dilemmas and make choices. One of the most intriguing and heart-wrenching episodes involves the conflict generated by Bo's turning over $100 to a homeless man, an act his father cannot understand, much less approve. Read the October 25 letter to Larry, pages 51 to 56 aloud, and discuss what happens. Why did Bo give the man the money? Was he right? Why is his dad so upset? Then, for a great lesson in persuasive writing, ask students to write a paper defending either Bo's position or his dad's. Those who choose Dad's side may wish to write in first person. For that matter, consider writing from the perspective of the man who got the money. What did it mean to *him*? Did it make a difference?

Curry, Barbara K. and James Michael Brodie. *Sweet Words So Brave: The Story of African American Literature*. Illustrated by Jerry Butler. 1996. Madison, WI: Zino Press. ISBN: 1-55933-179-8.

PICTURE BOOK/BIOGRAPHY/HISTORY (MIDDLE SCHOOL, HIGH SCHOOL)

SUMMARY: Through a creative collage of text, photographs, vibrant background colors, and striking oil paintings, Curry and Brodie bring to life the history, the courage, and the voice of America's finest African American writers. Within this text, history sings, moves, and breathes. Use this book as a fine example of ideas clearly presented; information enlivened by voice; and richness of detail. Also use it as a fine example of informational layout and presentation.

LESSON IDEA: Read samples of the book aloud. Invite students to explore others. Share samples of collage expression from other books as well to give students a sense of the range this form of writing can take. Collage is a *powerful* means of expression. Invite students, individually or in pairs/teams, to create a cultural collage celebrating their heritage and current cultural lifestyle. Collages might include combinations of poetry, expository writing (including history), bits of song lyrics, quotations from famous writers or artists, samples of art, sketches, and photographs, or any other representative pieces students may wish to incorporate. Display the results and/or present orally, with accompanying music or poetry readings.

Deary, Terry and Peter Hepplewhite. *Horrible Histories:*
The Awesome Egyptians. **1996. New York: Scholastic.**
ISBN: 0-590-03168-6.

NONFICTION HISTORY FOR FUN (MIDDLE SCHOOL, HIGH SCHOOL)

Ideas
19

SUMMARY: Deary's books are tough to categorize. They're history, all right, but surely not that dry, tedious stuff most of us remember. Deary and Hepplewhite are masters at digging out the most intriguing details available on any group, and though you wouldn't use their books as a core of your curriculum, you won't want to be without them, either, for they allow you to bring in the bits of information that make ancient people seem real. Did you know Egyptians lived mostly on bread and onions? Would not eat pork? Wore more make-up than we do? Could only have kings—not queens—so that queens had to dress as men, including wearing beards? Often married at age 12 or younger? This little book (only 128 pages) is packed with fascinating information. It's full of voice, too, so you'll remember what you read.

LESSON IDEA: Deary and Hepplewhite include a number of self-quizzes in their books, and this adds to the fun. You can give these orally to students prior to sharing selected passages. Then, invite students to imitate this self-quiz idea, based on the Deary-Hepplewhite books or on *anything* you're reading. Point out that beginning with a quiz is a great way to set up an oral presentation or a written report. It engages readers immediately (and ensures that the writer must know his/her stuff!)

See also

The Vile Victorians
The Blitzed Brits
The Vicious Vikings
The Rotten Romans

Diamond, Jared. *Guns, Germs, and Steel: The Fates of Human*
Societies. **1997. New York: W. W. Norton and Company.**
ISBN: 0-393-31755-2.

HISTORY/PHILOSOPHY/SCIENCE CHAPTER BOOK (HIGH SCHOOL)

SUMMARY: A sweeping, breathtaking summary of 13,000 years of human history from a brilliant writer who refuses to accept racial explanations for cultural differences. Why, he asks, didn't the Incas (to cite one example) invent guns and swords, mount themselves on horseback, invent ocean going ships and set about conquering the world? There are, Diamond tells us, explanations for such questions, but we must dig deeply to find them, and whatever your current views of world history, you're likely to find them both challenged and enriched by a 425-page book that is humbling and electrifying in its scope and depth. Diamond looks at history through the eyes of the history makers, examining issues from technology to livestock, religion to the spread of disease. A masterpiece of synthesis.

LESSON IDEA: You can use this book in many ways—asking students to try answering some of the provocative questions Diamond poses is perhaps the most obvious. But because this author writes with such style, encourage students to compare passages from Diamond's book to the information found in other sources, and to evaluate both for completeness, thoroughness of support and research, and skill in reaching an audience. What differences do your students see? What makes a book like Diamond's (a history book, after all) a best seller? A prize winner? **Extension:** For those students who take time to examine the book in some detail, pose this persuasive writing question: If you were on the committee to award the Pulitzer Prize for this book, would you vote to do so? Why or why not? (The same question may be asked of other books as well, of course.)

Edwards, Pamela Duncan. *Barefoot: Escape on the Underground Railroad*. Illustrated by Henry Cole. 1996. New York: HarperCollins Publishers. ISBN: **0-06-027137-X.**

HISTORY-BASED FICTIONAL PICTURE BOOK (PRIMARY THROUGH HIGH SCHOOL)

SUMMARY: A brilliant book for illustrating the concept of perspective, with chillingly realistic insight about how it must feel to be a slave on the run with death at your heels. In this book, we see the world through the eyes of forest animals: they see the bare feet of the escaped slave, the boots of the pursuers. This is an adventure story, but one based on historical fact. No matter the age of the students, if you're studying the underground railroad, this is a good place to begin. Younger students will simply enjoy the tension of a good story.

LESSON IDEA: How does a story look, sound, and feel from two different perspectives? Think of something as simple as leaving the house for school this morning. How might that story sound told through the eyes of a pet? The neighbor's dog? A bird perched outside the window? An ant hiding out on your kitchen countertop? Ask students to try telling the story, as it happened, in simple terms first. Then, tell it from the perspective of someone looking on and listening in. Which version is more interesting? Why?

Fox, Mem. *Wilfrid Gordon McDonald Partridge.* **Illustrated by Julie Vivas. 1985. New York: Kane/Miller Book Publishers. ISBN: 0-916291-26-X.**

PICTURE BOOK (PRIMARY THROUGH HIGH SCHOOL)

SUMMARY: Perhaps the greatest picture book ever written on making connections. Wilfrid Gordon and Miss Nancy—decades apart in age—become friends because each is so sensitive to the other's needs. Together, they explore memories and the ways in which the things we treasure keep us connected to our thoughts, recollections, hopes, and dreams.

LESSON IDEA: Have you ever asked students to write about a favorite object, gotten just a physical description, and said, "Where's the *meaning*? Where's the *depth*?" Ask students to bring in one favorite treasure: it might be a photograph, a gift, or a simple thing found on an outing, not purchased in a store at all (e.g., special rock, seashell). Have students meet in small groups of 3 or 4 to share their special treasures and the memories that go with them. Then, share Mem's book aloud. Talk about the memory connection, and ask each student to write about the meaning *behind* the object. Younger students can do pictures and dictate stories. You might accompany older students' writings with sketches or photos and make a class book of memories.

Gendler, Ruth. *The Book of Qualities.* **1988. New York: HarperCollins Publishers. ISBN: 0-06-096252-6.**

CREATIVE ESSAYS ON HUMAN QUALITIES (MIDDLE SCHOOL, HIGH SCHOOL)

SUMMARY: A fascinating, unique look at how an abstract idea (or any idea) can be defined through personification. Gendler takes a collection of 99 human traits and transforms them into personalities. Her imagination makes these one- and two-page essays sheer pleasure to read: e.g., "Intuition confessed that she has a 'spotty employment record.' She was fired from her last job for daydreaming." Both you and your students will enjoy exploring Gendler's highly creative creations, and then, perhaps, trying some of your own.

LESSON IDEA: Personification is a great vehicle for exploring truth in depth. How do we *really* see something? Gendler picks human traits. You might do the same; imitation is one great learning strategy. Or get brave and try colors, months, years, states or cities, letters of the alphabet, names, kinds of trees or flowers, foods, automobiles, or anything that strikes your fancy. How about the six traits? How does Voice dress? How does Conventions enter the room? How does Organization throw a dinner party? Be sure to share results aloud. It's half the fun. This writing can be a group activity.

Haley, Jan. J. Rooker, manatee. Illustrated by Paul Brent. 1996. Bemidji, MN: Focus Publishing. ISBN: 1-885904-05-3.

Ideas 22

NONFICTION PICTURE BOOK (ELEMENTARY, MIDDLE SCHOOL)

SUMMARY: How do you take the information you've gathered through research and weave it into your writing, thereby enriching the ideas? Author Jan Haley shows us exactly how in this beautifully illustrated nonfiction story of a young manatee's rescue off the coast of Florida. Haley's book is fact-based; in addition, her preface and a section entitled "More About Manatees" at the end provide additional important information.

LESSON IDEA: Ask students first what they know, or *think* they know, about manatees. Make a list. Now ask what they'd *like* to know. List questions. After reading the book, check the accuracy of previous information, and also check to see what questions were answered. How much information did Haley pack into her book? Maybe she stopped short of answering *every* question. When is enough *enough*? Now let student writers try their own hands at crafting a piece of writing based on research (on manatees or *any* topic). Let the writing take any form: a poster, a brochure for a new zoo exhibit, a newspaper or journal article, a series of informational pieces that walk visitors through an aquarium exhibit, a short textbook chapter, etc. Begin with a list of questions an audience might have. Then, talk about ways to whittle down lots of information so it fits the needs of an audience and does not overwhelm them.

Isaacson, Philip M. *A Short Walk Around the Pyramids and Through the World of Art*. 1993. New York: Alfred A. Knopf, Inc. ISBN: 0-679-81523-6.

ART COLLECTION/INFORMATIONAL CHAPTER BOOK (PRIMARY THROUGH HIGH SCHOOL)

SUMMARY: Here's a lesson on how to make a complex subject simple. This book is the very essence of good informational writing: clear, complete, engaging, penetrable, unpretentious. The question is, *How can a writer teach so much—and teach it so well—in so few words?* Of course, he uses pictures, too. They help! But the writing is extraordinary: clear, lean, informative. Just reading aloud from this book (pick a section!) is a lesson in itself, but if you want more . . .

LESSON IDEA: Ask students to select one piece of art: any piece, any period. Ask them to describe it in an analytical style that helps the reader understand the piece. They might refer to color, imagery, mood, shape, movement, use of lighting, or anything else striking. Research (to see what others have said) is fine, but the writing should also reflect the student's own response to the piece. For a real challenge, keep the piece between 200 to 400 words, no more. Make every word work! Fill the piece with detail.

Jones, Charlotte Foltz. *Accidents May Happen: Fifty Inventions Discovered By Mistake*. 1996. New York: Delacorte Press. ISBN: 0-385-32240-2.

NONFICTION HISTORY OF INVENTIONS (ELEMENTARY, MIDDLE SCHOOL)

SUMMARY: How did toasted cereal come to be? Who accidentally dried out the first raisin? Why do we have buttons on our jackets? Who stumbled onto the concept of liquid paper? Fingerprinting? Photography? Dynamite? Find out in this highly entertaining collection of historical accidents that have changed our lives in dramatic ways. A great read-aloud book with a wonderful cohesive theme: many creative inventions pop up while the inventor is trying to do something else. (Excellent for organization, too, because of its common theme approach.)

LESSON IDEA: Have fun asking students to think of how inventions—take the yo-yo, for example—might have come about. They can guess orally, or write a short guess to share in a group. Then, you can read the actual history, likely to be more bizarre than any of the guesses. Older writers may wish to follow up with additional research on a given invention—fingerprints, for instance.

See also the following books with a similar theme:

- Jones, Charlotte Foltz. *Mistakes That Worked.*
- Jones, Charlotte Foltz. *Fingerprints and Talking Bones.*

Krull, Kathleen. *Lives of the Writers: Comedies, Tragedies and What the Neighbors Thought*. 1994. San Diego: Harcourt Brace & Company. ISBN: 0-15-248009-9.

BIOGRAPHICAL CHAPTER BOOK (ELEMENTARY THROUGH HIGH SCHOOL)

SUMMARY: "Two days after his twelfth birthday, in a damp factory overrun with rats, Charles Dickens went to work to support his family. All day, with two meal breaks (often raisin pudding with a penny loaf of bread) he pasted labels on bottles of black shoe polish." What fun Charles had as a child! Rarely will you find a better book for bringing famous writers to life. The biographies are short, but full of just the sorts of things you would have wanted to know had you been their neighbors.

LESSON IDEA: A simple way to use this book, of course, is to read sections aloud before you read or discuss the literature of a given writer, then talk about how his or her life might show up in the writing. (Doesn't sound too hard to make the connection with Dickens, does it?) You can extend this, of course, by asking students to research other writers, or if you want to get a little trickier, ask students to *become* the writers, and to use their research to do an autobiographical piece from each writer's point of view, or an interview/press conference with the class.

Kuralt, Charles. *Charles Kuralt's America*. 1995. New York: G.P. Putnam's Sons. ISBN: 0-399-14083-2.

NONFICTION TRAVELOGUE (MIDDLE SCHOOL, HIGH SCHOOL)

SUMMARY: If you could have traveled the United States with one guide, you might have wished it to be Charles Kuralt, a man who knew the value of small things from daffodil bulbs to the cry of the wild loon echoing over a morning mist-covered lake. This is a GREAT read-aloud book, but be selective; it's long.

LESSON IDEA: Use this book as a lead-in to descriptive writing pieces on students' own community. Allow some variety here, from the chapter approach that Kuralt uses to poems, pamphlets and travel brochures, newspaper pieces, reviews of local restaurants and hotels or tourist spots. Let your imaginations break free.

Macaulay, David. *The New Way Things Work*. 1998. New York: Houghton Mifflin. ISBN: 0-395-93847-3.

ILLUSTRATED LISTING OF MODERN MACHINES AND HOW THEY WORK (ELEMENTARY THROUGH HIGH SCHOOL)

SUMMARY: Ever wonder how the brakes on your car work, or why they *don't*? Wonder how helicopters fly? What static electricity has to do with your photocopy machine? How an automatic transmission works or why smoke detectors fail to go off? If you're curious about any of these or similar questions, here's your book. A technical book fit for browsing. Not a simple thing to write, but Macaulay has done it. If you teach tech writing in any form, this book belongs in your class, for any number of reasons. It's clear, concise, entertaining, and brilliantly illustrated: in short, it's all the things good tech writing should be.

LESSON IDEA: Share several of Macaulay's passages; let students decide which ones you will share. Then, invite them to create informational brochures or posters on any simple tool around the house. A pair of scissors, a rubber band, a paper clip, etc. (For more of a challenge, take on something complex, such as a radio, microwave oven, remote controller, video camera, etc.) Recommend some research prior to writing to answer questions such as who invented the object and when. But also encourage students to do their own experimenting in answering basic questions such as, "What is this object good for? How will it help us in twenty-first century America—if at all? Will it soon be obsolete?" All presentations should be short and to the point, but should contain enough information to satisfy a curious reader, as well as illustrations to show the workings, normal use, plus any moving parts.

MacLachlan, Patricia. *All the Places to Love*. Illustrated by Mike Wimmer. 1994. New York: HarperCollins Publishers. ISBN: **0-06-021098-2.**

PICTURE BOOK (ELEMENTARY, MIDDLE SCHOOL)

SUMMARY: The places in this warm, nostalgic book boast no parking lots or neon signs. They're those places of the heart known only to the writer: the inside of grandfather's barn, the top of the hill, the place where the old turtle crosses the path. The book is an open invitation to students to discover and celebrate places that carve individual and sacred memories in the mind.

LESSON IDEA: This book is a perfect opener for descriptive writing. After reading the book aloud, invite students first to brainstorm a list of important personal places. Share lists aloud so students hear one another's ideas; it triggers more memories. Ask them to add to their lists as they hear ideas they like. Then, ask them to choose one that stands out. List all sensory details (sights, sounds, smells, tastes, feelings) they associate with that place. Now, write a description so vivid it will put the reader right at the spot. Create a class book: *All the Places to Remember.*

MacLachlan, Patricia. *What You Know First*. Illustrated by Barry Moser. 1995. New York: HarperCollins Publishers. ISBN: **0-06-024413-5.**

PICTURE BOOK (PRIMARY THROUGH HIGH SCHOOL)

SUMMARY: For many students—not to mention adults—the very thought of moving is traumatic. How do you leave all that is your home, yet retain a sense of your own identity? Imagine yourself leaving all that you know to go to a strange environment. What might you take along to remind you of home? MacLachlan's book explores this theme in a sensitive, nostalgic way.

LESSON IDEA: Prior to sharing the book, talk about the notion of moving. What emotions does it evoke? Excitement? Anticipation? Anxiety? Also talk about various kinds of moves: to a new home, new school, new grade level, or new sports team. Then, as you read the book, ask students to listen carefully for the things the young girl in the story decides to take with her. Why does she make the choices she does? What do her choices tell about her? Ask students to think about what they might take with them if they were to move. They can draw pictures of their choices, or better still, bring in examples so you can make a display. As a follow-up, ask each student to talk or write about his/her choices.

Martin, Jacqueline Briggs. *Snowflake Bentley.* **Illustrated by Mary Azarian. 1998. New York: Houghton Mifflin. ISBN: 0-395-86162-4.**

FACT-BASED PICTURE BOOK (ELEMENTARY, MIDDLE SCHOOL)

SUMMARY: This is the true story of Vermont-born Wilson Bentley, who made the study of snowflakes his life's work. He was among the first to discover that snowflakes, while universally six-sided, are unique-—and once melted, will not return to us in the same pattern, ever. This is an excellent text for showing how narrative and informational writing can blend beautifully, and how each enriches the other. Writing modes really are not exclusive; sometimes, a story is the best way to make a point!

LESSON IDEA: Notice the intriguing format of this book; the main text tells the story, but the sidebars fill in important historical information. You might invite your students to try this format when they wish or need to blend narrative with informational writing. They will learn not only the differences in purpose, but also something about making one form harmonize with the other.

Moss, Marissa. *Rachel's Journal.* **1998. San Diego: Harcourt Brace and Company. ISBN: 0-15-201806-9.**

FACT-BASED FICTIONAL JOURNAL (ELEMENTARY, MIDDLE SCHOOL)

SUMMARY: Though 10-year-old Rachel is not a real person, every adventure documented in her fascinating journal really happened to *someone* heading west on the Oregon trail. Not only are the details fascinating, but the research behind this work is impressive. The book is an excellent example of how much research enlivens and supports even good fictional writing. The voice is strong, and Rachel emerges as an intriguing, spunky character who will win the hearts of your students.

LESSON IDEA: As a warm-up, you might give students a U.S. map and ask them if they can trace the path of the Oregon trail. Then, let them compare their best guesses with the actual trail so beautifully illustrated on the inside cover of this exceptional book. How close did they come? How many cities along the way have your students visited? Next, read the book aloud, a chapter at a time, asking students to document the things they learn about the trek west along the Oregon trail. After each reading, invite students to meet briefly (3–5 minutes) in small groups to compare notes and see which details each noticed (the book is very rich with historical information, and no one note-taker will get it all, so comparing is helpful). **Follow-up:** Ask students to write a journal entry or series of entries from any period in history, including the future! They should expect to cite at least two sources of factual information, showing that their journals, though fictional, are based on real-life happenings (futuristic journals, of course, will be hypothetical but can still be based on current scientific research).

Ideas
27

Myers, Walter Dean. *Monster.* 1999. New York: HarperCollins Publishers. ISBN: 0-06-028077-8.

YOUNG ADULT FICTION (HIGH SCHOOL)

SUMMARY: A disarmingly realistic and haunting portrayal of a black ghetto youth's terrifying experience being arrested and tried for felony murder. The story itself is riveting. But the frosting on the cake is what Myers does with the format. It's brilliant. He alternates sections from Steve Harmon's personal diary with Steve's vision of his life *as a movie.* This is Steve's way to cope: to see what is happening to him as a film. He includes stage directions and spoken parts, as in a real script. As students read, they must figure out for themselves what things like VO (voice-over) and CU (close-up) mean. Even more interesting is when and how Steve chooses to film things as he does. Focusing in on one character or scene versus another (by simply moving the camera) can be a powerful way of changing the whole emphasis of a story.

LESSON IDEA: If you have video equipment available for students to use, excellent. But if not, use Myers' book as a model to help students think visually. First, share a portion of the book aloud and discuss it (so they can understand how it is set up), then allow them to continue reading to themselves, reminding them to pay special attention to close-ups and camera angles. Ask students to take *one* of their own narratives and to rewrite all or a portion of it as if it were a script, attending to lighting, camera angles and ranges, and dialogue. (Note that most of Myers' story is told via dialogue.) **Extension:** This also makes a fine group activity, in which students work together on a short narrative, then present the results as a play or reader's theater. If video equipment is available, they may wish to produce a short (5 to 10-minute) video of their story.

**Nye, Bill. *The Science Guy's Big Blast of Science*. 1993.
Reading, MA: Addison Wesley Longman.**
ISBN: **0-201-60864-2.**

INFORMATIONAL ESSAYS ON PHYSICAL SCIENCE (ELEMENTARY, MIDDLE SCHOOL)

SUMMARY: Bill Nye has a gift. He studied science at Cornell under Carl Sagan and has won 11 Emmys. But best of all, Bill can take an abstract, difficult concept and translate it into simple, conversational language so you "get it." The selections are *short* and snappy, the language lively and precise. You can easily use this book to teach appropriate voice and word choice in informational writing; also use it to illustrate clarity, and its importance in writing that leans toward the technical side.

LESSON IDEA: Give students some practice in *writing* for clarity. Read at least five of Nye's samples aloud, and if possible, provide written copies for students to mark up and use as models during the lesson. Ask them to note phrases or techniques Bill Nye uses to make meaning clear. Discuss his strategies (e.g., use of metaphor) as a class; list them. Then, provide students with a piece written in *slightly* more technical language (or in vague, unclear language); you might pull a piece from a textbook or from a science journal or how-to manual of any kind. Look for a short piece that does not demand in-depth understanding of the topic—but one that also is not very well-written. Ask students, individually or in pairs, to rewrite the piece using some of Bill Nye's strategies for ensuring clarity. Share a few results aloud, commenting on revision strategies that seemed to work best.

**Nye, Bill. *Bill Nye the Science Guy's Big Blue Ocean*. 1999.
New York: Hyperion Books for Children.** ISBN: **078685063-9.**

SCIENCE CHAPTER BOOK (ELEMENTARY, MIDDLE SCHOOL)

SUMMARY: This book is so visually appealing, you could easily use it to illustrate layout. It's a veritable feast of photos, cartoons, sketches, lists, charts and text, a real tribute to modern informational writing. Bill Nye, the NASA scientist, could easily show off but he Never does. He strives to make everything crystal clear, whether writing about the food web, the role of salt, or plate tectonics. You won't say, "Huh?" and you won't be bored, either. Here's a book that mixes life science and physical science beautifully.

LESSON IDEA: If you enjoy science, the lessons are built in: "12 killer experiments." You can make a tsunami in your bathtub, learn to defend yourself as a squid would, or test how far away you could smell things if you were a shark. Of course, you can ask students to write up results if you wish—or to present their experiments. Either way, they'll gain a powerful introduction to good informational/technical writing. And Nye makes it painless.

O'Brien, Tim. *The Things They Carried.* **1991. New York: Penguin Books.** ISBN: **0-14-014773-X.**

FACT-BASED NOVEL/MEMOIR (HIGH SCHOOL)

SUMMARY: This has been called the greatest book ever written about Vietnam. Vivid, moving, enlightening, and provocative, it makes you feel that you are right there, living it. You will surely experience the horror, and the total life changes that war brings. It is unflinching and graphic (and the language may be offensive to some), but it also probes deeply into the mental anguish and numbness of those who must learn to live in a war zone.

LESSON IDEA: The title of this book is an invitation to reflection. It essentially asks the question, "What do the things we carry tell about us?" The answer, of course is "almost everything." Here's an opportunity to do character analysis through possessions. Begin by reading Chapter 1 (or some part thereof), "The Things They Carried," aloud. Students may wish to make notes on items they recall and why. Next, divide students into groups and ask each group to assemble—perhaps in an old backpack, briefcase, or even a wallet or paper bag—a collection of items that might belong to one character, male or female, any age, in any place. Don't feel locked in to a military context. Use the items to create a character profile. Before sharing the profile with the class, ask other students what conclusions they might draw from the items. Compare their analysis to what the group came up with. **Extension:** Ask students to do a personal analysis based on what they themselves carry. What do the items tell about them? This is more fun, of course, if you model it first, showing three or four items *you* routinely carry, and discussing (with help from students) what each tells about you.

O'Dell, Scott. *My Name Is Not Angelica.* **1989. New York: Houghton Mifflin Company.** ISBN: **0-395-51061-9.**

YOUNG ADULT HISTORICAL NOVEL (MIDDLE SCHOOL)

SUMMARY: Raisha, a Senegalese girl and daughter of a chief, is brought as a slave to the Danish owned Caribbean island of St. John, where she is auctioned off like any piece of art or machinery, and enters a world she could not have imagined in her native land. An honest look at the cruelty of slavery, and the inevitable uprising of 1733, as witnessed by a daring young woman whose spirit would not be crushed. An adventurous, compelling tale, based on true events.

LESSON IDEA: Two things make O'Dell's book work particularly well. One is the vivid portrayal of realistic characters, each of whom has his/her own motivation. The book is an excellent one, therefore, to use in discussing motivation, or what drives characters to do what they do. The other is the enormous, in-depth research that O'Dell put into this book to be sure his details were authentic. Ask students to focus on any time in history, and using at least three sources for information, to try to identify what everyday life was like during that time. Then, portray, through a story, letter or journal entry, one day in the life of a character who might have lived during that time. Students must rely on sufficient research to bring the time to life. In addition, it is helpful if the character is motivated to achieve a goal or overcome a difficulty.

Quammen, David. *Wild Thoughts from Wild Places*. 1998. New York: Scribner. ISBN: 0-684-83509-6.

VIC'S PICKS SCIENCE ESSAYS (HIGH SCHOOL)

SUMMARY: Award-winning naturalist and science writer David Quammen roams the world in search of new information and new perspectives on the many species that share our earth. From the coyotes of Los Angeles to the white tigers of the Cincinnati Zoo, you will find his subjects highly entertaining and provocative. Quammen is not one to hold his viewpoints in check, and for this reason, his essays make an excellent basis for illustrating and stimulating good persuasive writing.

LESSON IDEA: Choose one essay and invite students to write a persuasive essay answering one question prompted by that essay. You can let students come up with their own questions. For example, in "To Live and Die in L.A.," Quammen suggests that coyotes are more like us than are many primates. Good questions might be, Is this true? If so, how? He also shows how the coyote has adapted to life in a crowded human-dominated environment, so another question might be, How does the coyote do it? Of course, not everyone likes dealing with coyotes—who have done in many a small pet, and who do not mind stealing food right off the grill. Are they entertaining innovators or renegades to be hunted? Read an essay and watch the questions flow.

Ringgold, Faith. *Aunt Harriet's Underground Railroad in the Sky.*
1993. New York: Crown Publishers. ISBN: 0-517-88543-3.

Ideas
31

HISTORY-BASED PICTURE BOOK (ELEMENTARY, MIDDLE SCHOOL)

SUMMARY: A wonderful companion piece for *Barefoot: Escape on the Underground Railroad* (Pamela Duncan Edwards, this section). Here young Cassie and her brother Be Be take an imaginary trip on a railroad in the sky—and learn from Aunt Harriet Tubman what the underground railroad was all about, and how many people risked their lives to flee slavery or to help those on the run for their lives. It's history combined, thanks to Ringgold's story telling talent, with the glamour and appeal of a fairy tale.

LESSON IDEA: You might follow Ringgold's own suggestion at the end of the book. After reading both Ringgold's story and the true history of Harriet Tubman herself, have students create from paper an underground "train" that tells the story of how the underground railroad worked. (Directions are given in the book.) Follow up with a discussion on how the term "underground railroad" came to be. You might have students do a first write, exploring their ideas on this, then following up with some research on the origin of the term. Why is "underground railroad" so appropriate when in reality it was neither a train nor underground?

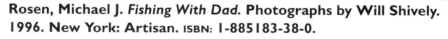

Rosen, Michael J. *Fishing With Dad.* **Photographs by Will Shively.**
1996. New York: Artisan. ISBN: 1-885183-38-0.

NONFICTION BLANK VERSE WITH PHOTOS (PRIMARY THROUGH HIGH SCHOOL)

SUMMARY: Remember fishing as a kid? If you do, picture yourself telling a story about it. If you don't—well, picture it anyway. What kinds of details would you include? Where you went? What you used for bait? What kind of fish you caught? This is a book that shows you how to go from generalities to tiny, visual details that put you right there: ". . . one of the lines whines a high *eeeee* . . . and I feel it slide between my fingers. The bobber dunks, then zips, unzips! zigzags across the waves, and the fishing pole—I grab it just in time— doesn't just bounce, it bows down and points to the water, as if to say, *right here!*" *See?* You *are* there. You are fishing.

LESSON IDEA: Ask students to do a brief outline version of a "fishing story." It doesn't need to focus on fishing. It can be *any* narrative. They should keep it short, skimpy, sketchy. And here's the trick: Write on every other line, and on ONE side of the paper only. Leave LOTS of room on the righthand side as well as between the lines to add detail. Now, prior to their revisions, read *Fishing With Dad* and talk about the kinds of details Rosen uses to bring his memories to life. Then, ask students to revise their papers on the righthand side of the page, adding "Rosen-esque" details that will put the reader at the scene. Share results in groups, if you like.

Rowling, J. K. *Harry Potter and the Sorcerer's Stone*. 1997. New York: Scholastic. ISBN: 0-590-353403.

FANTASY CHAPTER BOOK (ELEMENTARY, MIDDLE SCHOOL)

SUMMARY: Nothing terribly scary happens in this book, but it always seems as if it's *about* to, which is what keeps us turning the pages. The whole idea of a school just for witches and wizards is appealing to begin with, though older readers will notice numerous alarming (and humorous) analogies to real-life school. All the fun of Hansel and Gretel in a tale updated to fit modern readers. Action, adventure, humor, suspense, and just a dollop of danger—though you know darn well old Harry will come through. What more could you ask? Bring on the sequels (an eventual total of *seven* books are scheduled for print). Rowling has been compared to P. L. Travers and Roald Dahl; the comparison is good; she's a master teller of tales. You have to pay attention, though: lots of new terminology!

LESSON IDEA: Character development is an essential component of ideas. If you share this book as a read-aloud, you can have fun asking students to choose one character from the book and keeping a running journal during the time of the reading. Not *every* student needs to pick a different character, but there are many intriguing and unusual characters in this book: Harry, Fred, Ron, Dudley, Miss Hooch, Hagrid, Hermione, Snape, Malfoy, Professor McGonagall. So you can get a *wide* variety. As you go, invite a few of your students to share all or part of their journal entries, a good way of predicting where the story is about to go next! **Alternatives:** How about an advertisement for the school? Or: An interview with one of the "celebrity" teachers that might appear in the local paper . . . A menu from the dining room . . . A map showing the layout of the school . . . Snape's will . . . McGonagall's shopping list for the holidays . . . A lesson plan from one of the teachers . . . Let your imagination soar.

Seinfeld, Jerry. *SeinLanguage*. 1993. New York: Bantam Books. ISBN: 0-553-56915-5.

VIC'S PICKS

SATIRICAL ESSAYS ON LIFE (MIDDLE SCHOOL, HIGH SCHOOL)

SUMMARY: This is one to reach for when students say, "I haven't been to China and my goldfish didn't die, so I have nothing to write about."

Like Seinfeld's old comedy series, this book makes the point that everyday life is story-worthy. You do NOT need to write about world peace or how to deal with global warming; Jerry writes about dry cleaning, soap on a rope, cookies, phone machines, battles for parking spaces, the doctor's waiting room, the tedium of picking out a "little outfit" to wear for the day, and a hundred other little curiosities and annoyances. You'll need to censor a bit. <u>Not all pieces are sharable with students</u>—but *most* are. So, have fun suggesting the joy of the tiny topic.

LESSON IDEA: Instead of writing immediately, begin a class notebook of ideas for "tiny topics." You might brainstorm a list of categories first: e.g., irritations, things to appreciate, things that cost too much, things you would definitely make against the law if you could, things no one can remember, things around the house we don't need anymore, things neighbors should *not* be allowed to do, and so on. Put them on butcher paper and post them so students can add to the list any time they feel like it. After a week or two, have each student choose <u>one</u> topic to write about. Join in the fun and write with them. Have a "Tiny Topic Day" and share the results.

Shaw, Nancy. *Sheep Out to Eat*. Illustrated by Margot Apple. 1992. New York: Houghton Mifflin Company. ISBN: 0-395-72027-3.

PICTURE BOOK (PRIMARY, ELEMENTARY, MIDDLE SCHOOL)

SUMMARY: Though the language is extraordinarily simple, this is a hoot of a book to share aloud with younger reader-writers. It's sensitive, clever, and a sheer delight. Students will love the rhyme, the humor, and the *very* funny pictures. If you work with older students, have a look at the lesson idea that follows to see how to turn a fairly simple text into a detail-building activity.

LESSON IDEA: First, read the book. Then divide the text into parts for six to nine groups, depending on your class size. It is best to have three or four students in each group. You'll notice there are three sheep in the group; give them names. Then, in individual groups, work on filling in details to expand and develop the story. You can offer some suggestions: e.g., putting in some dialogue, sharing feelings. (What author/teacher Barry Lane calls sharing "thoughtshots," or what you think, and "snapshots," or what you see.) When you finish re-writing, do a read-around to see how much detail groups have added to the story. In what ways is it different? How does detail enrich writing? By the way, who is your audience now?

Solheim, James. *It's Disgusting and We Ate It! True Food Facts From Around the World and Throughout History.* **Illustrated by Eric Brace. 1998. New York: Simon and Schuster. ISBN: 0-689-80675-2.**

NONFICTION PICTURE BOOK (ELEMENTARY, MIDDLE SCHOOL)

SUMMARY: Amazing, not-for-the-squeamish facts about the many foods we, and others, actually eat! Fried robins on toast! No! Yes—they're not kidding. Dare to look in your fridge? Want to know how cheese is made? How about hot dogs? Want a taste of 40,000-year-old mammoth stew? Earthworm soup? Sidewinder salad? Your students will *delight* in every page, illustrations and all. Is *this* the idea of research? To look up fascinating information and teach people new things?

LESSON IDEA: This book is a true research winner because it includes a recommended additional reading list (p. 35) and bibliography (p. 36)—not to mention one of the wackiest indexes ever (p. 37). The result? You can assign further research, having students work individually or in pairs. What a wonderful way to begin learning about a new country or culture, starting with what they eat, *or* find repulsive. Students may be amazed to learn that some of their favorites are considered disgusting in other parts of the world. Organize some research around food, and present it in a variety of formats, including reports, ads, poems, recipes, brochures, menus, or, if you're brave, some real samples.

Thomas, Lewis. *The Medusa and the Snail: More Notes of a Biology Watcher.* **1995. New York: Penguin Books. ISBN: 0-14-024319-4.**

NONFICTION ESSAYS (MIDDLE SCHOOL, HIGH SCHOOL)

SUMMARY: Thomas will make you fall in love with topics you thought would put you to sleep: warts, punctuation, serving on a committee, or "Why Montaigne Is Not a Bore." Sound interesting? You might be surprised. Thomas has a way of enthralling his audience. His words, voice, and originality all beckon. Surely this is what good informational/technical writing is about—to make an audience wake up and call for more.

LESSON IDEA: Group students into 3s or 4s. Pass out 3 × 5 notecards. Ask each person, without showing his/her topic to anyone else in the group, to write on one side of the notecard the most boring topic he or she can think of to write about. Allow a few minutes for reflection on this. Now, pass the notecards one person to the left. Ask the next student to read the topic he/she has just received, and on the *opposite* side of the notecard, to write three *intriguing* questions he or she would like answered pertaining to this topic. Return cards to original writers and share the questions, to show there is audience interest in

just about anything. There really *are* no boring topics, just bored writers!
Extension: After sharing questions, instead of returning the cards, pass them one more person to the left. Ask that person to use one of the questions as a prompt for a good lead. Share leads with the whole class.

Van Allsburg, Chris. *The Mysteries of Harris Burdick.* **1984. Boston: Houghton Mifflin. ISBN: 0-395-35393-9.**

MINIMAL-TEXT PICTURE BOOK (ELEMENTARY THROUGH HIGH SCHOOL)

SUMMARY: A book that has become a classic. Mysterious pictures drawn by Harris Burdick and left in the home of Peter Wenders tug at our imaginations. Supposedly, each had a story written to accompany it, but alas, the stories have been lost, leaving us, if we wish, to invent our own. The pictures range from humorous to mysterious to whimsical. Most students find them fascinating, and find it quite easy to choose one as a launching point for a good story.

LESSON IDEA: For variety, let students work in pairs or groups to interpret a picture of their choice and write something—anything—based upon it. We tend to think "story," but these pictures are too good to be that restrictive. Students could do letters, business correspondence, resumes, wills, sets of directions, journals, advertisements, or any kind of writing connecting somehow to the picture. If you do this as a group activity, you might ask each person within the group to compose a different form of writing (e.g., one resume, one letter, one journal, and so on), making sure they are interconnected and all relate to one picture. This is a good lesson on how writing can play many roles within each person's life, and how multiple forms of writing can create a more complete picture of a "happening" than can narrative alone.

Warren, Andrea. *Orphan Train Rider: One Boy's True Story.* **1996. Boston: Houghton Mifflin. ISBN: 0-395-91362-4.**

ILLUSTRATED CHAPTER BOOK (ELEMENTARY, MIDDLE SCHOOL)

SUMMARY: At the turn of the twentieth century, eastern parents were often too poor to keep their children (when a new baby came, the oldest had to leave, even if he/she was only seven or eight). Many were sent west on "orphan trains" to find homes. Despite painful memories, Lee Nailling, born in 1917, agreed to tell his tale. Through his recollections, tens of thousands of abandoned children find a voice at last. Author and researcher Andrea Warren tells her story in a steadfast, never-trembling manner, though it would be easy to cave in at the thought of small children trucked cross the country, pit-stopped in tiny towns, then forced to sit in rows for inspection of muscles, teeth, ears, posture. "I picked him because his hair was combed," one adoptive mother confessed. Many found themselves virtual indentured servants, taken in because someone needed a farm hand—for free. Lee felt lucky to find his new farm family; like others, he had left a world in which orphan children were publicly hanged for stealing food.

LESSON IDEA: So many writing possibilities emerge from this book that you may find yourself overwhelmed. Your students might put together any of the following: a diary of an orphan train rider, a poster advertising orphan children available for adoption, a list of rules that might have been posted in a 1900 orphanage, a letter of request written by someone wishing to adopt an orphan child, letters written back and forth between siblings adopted by different families, a journal kept by an adoptive parent, a newspaper person's account of one of the orphan train stops or the inspections held by prospective adoptive parents, an inspector's report of what he found upon investigating conditions in an orphanage, a newspaper account of a hanging for stealing food, a 1990 reflection by a former orphan train rider thinking back. More ideas will occur to you as you read this often startling book.

Wisniewski, David. *The Secret Knowledge of Grown-Ups*. 1998. New York: Lothrop, Lee & Shepard Books. ISBN: 0-688-15339-9.

PICTURE BOOK (ELEMENTARY, MIDDLE SCHOOL)

SUMMARY: An unusual book with a satirical tone, full of whimsy and fun. Everyone loves secrets—well, almost everyone. This is a book that lets us in on the secrets behind the rules grown-ups make kids live by. For instance, grown-ups like to make kids eat their vegetables. Why? Because they're good for you, right? Wrong!! The real reason, the secret reason, is that if we let them get out of hand, veggies would take over the world in a power struggle too ugly to contemplate. So—do your part. Keep that broccoli under control.

LESSON IDEA: Clever as he is, Wisniewski hasn't begun to exhaust all the possibilities. Brainstorm one or two rules your students (or you!) have had to live by. Then brainstorm the possible "real" reasons behind them. Don't try for logic here. The idea is to let your imagination soar. Make a class book of the secrets behind the rules—at home, school, in traffic, wherever, whenever. Remember—you have to come up with the "real" reason not everyone would think of! It's confidential. Shhhhhhh.

Wulffson, Don L. *When Human Heads Were Footballs: Surprising Stories of How Sports Began.* 1998. New York: Simon and Schuster. ISBN: 0-689-81959-5.

NONFICTION CHAPTER BOOK (MIDDLE SCHOOL, HIGH SCHOOL)

Ideas
37

SUMMARY: Was football really played first with human heads? Amazingly, yes. Later, cows' bladders were used, and when they were found not to hold up well, they were covered with animal hides, pigskin being the toughest. Perhaps you didn't know that during the Middle Ages football was called "townball," and that everyone played, with up to 200 people on a side. They played all over town, leaving both town and team in shambles. At the end of the game, both wounded and dead—yes, some players gave their life for the game!—were carted from the wreckage. This is a voicy, highly intriguing summary of the histories of many sports, from football to table tennis. If you have sports players or fans among your students, it's one nonfiction example you don't want to miss.

LESSON IDEA: Imagine yourself a player or observer in the days when one of these wild and wooly sports was getting its start. You might do an advertising poster or flyer, a news write-up of a game, a diary entry of your own participation, or a write-up from an observer's point of view. Several students who work on the same sport from different perspectives (player, fan, observer, sports writer) could do a small news letter.

VIC'S PICKS

Wyeth, Sharon Dennis. *Something Beautiful.* Illustrated by Chris K. Soentpiet. 1998. New York: Bantam Doubleday. ISBN: 0-385-32239-9.

PICTURE BOOK (PRIMARY THROUGH HIGH SCHOOL)

SUMMARY: Inspired by the author's own childhood memories, *Something Beautiful* tells the reflective, first-person story of a young girl who longs to see "something beautiful" in her life. It isn't easy. She lives amidst poverty, the homeless, metal fences, and graffiti. But she searches, and through her search, we too learn something about what beauty is. (This book makes a fine companion piece to Mem Fox's *Wilfrid Gordon McDonald Partridge,* this section.)

LESSON IDEA: Conduct your own class search for what is beautiful in life. Ask students to look for the less-than-obvious, as the heroine of *Something Beautiful* does—to see the world in a new and fresh way. When each of your students has written a paragraph (which can be illustrated) about one beautiful discovery, bind them into a class book for all to share.

Wyeth, Sharon Dennis. *Once on This River*. 1998. New York: Alfred A. Knopf, Inc. ISBN: 0-679-89446-2.

HISTORICAL NOVEL (MIDDLE SCHOOL)

SUMMARY: Eleven-year-old Monday de Groot knows little of the horrors of slavery when she embarks on a journey with her mother from Madagascar to New York in the mid 1700s. Monday's mother, however, has numerous secrets to be uncovered, including an intimate knowledge of slavery and a passionate desire to free her own enslaved brother. Her journey is a quest. It is both dangerous and fascinating. Through it, Monday—who helps deliver a baby on the very first page—develops a sense of self and courage that will rock readers to the core. Wyeth's book is extremely well researched and will hold young readers' attention while teaching them much about New York's early history—not everyone knows, for instance, that slaves lived and worked in this part of early America. This is a book rich with detail and voice, stunning in its honesty. The photographs of estate inventories (which include "owned" persons) and of advertisements for slaves to be sold are haunting, stark reminders of a not so distant brutality; and they add an authenticity to this fine work.

LESSON IDEA: This is an excellent text for showing students how to connect research and fiction—so often students think research is only for informational writing! Look closely at the documents that introduce each chapter—authentic documents taken from 1700s New York. Together, what do these documents show about the time in which Monday and her mother lived? How did people think? How did they do business? What moral or legal issues and beliefs guided their lives? Talk about how characters can grow out of an understanding of history as told through the documents of the time. You may wish to follow this up by assembling a collection of current documents that tell something about the time in which we live: contracts, advertisements, posters, research findings, headline news articles, photographs, etc. Create a class book, annotated, to show how culture is represented by the writings of the times—even such humble things as recipes or theater posters. **Extension:** This is a story told largely through dialogue. It is through the characters' words that we discover who they are and how they think. Ask students to create a short (one- to two-page) piece of dialogue in which the characters reveal their thinking and show their inner selves. They could choose characters from *Once on This River* or from another work—or combine the two. Some writers may wish to choose real life characters or to set up a dialogue between someone living now (say, an African-American author) and one of the characters from the book. What might they have to say to each other if they could converse across the years?

Books for Teaching

Organization

Once a writer has gathered information or put a story line together, it's time to think about organization: how to begin, where to go next, and how to end the piece. The books in this section feature the qualities key to sound organization: leads designed to hook a reader and keep his or her attention, sequencing that makes sense, strong transitions that link sentences or ideas together, and a solid conclusion that ties things together in the reader's mind—but often leaves the reader with something to think about, too. These books help expand what students have learned about the importance of clarity and detail by showing them how to put information together in an order that informs, persuades, or entertains a reader.

Teach organization by

- Working on leads (read aloud!)
- Working on transitions
- Working on endings (read these aloud, too!)
- Analyzing patterns in what you read
- Comparing the organization of different texts— say, a business letter and a short story

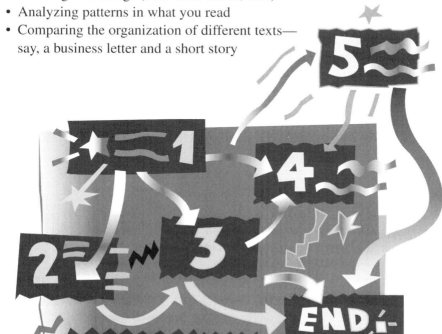

Blake, Quentin. *Zagazoo*. 1999. New York: Orchard Books.
ISBN: 0-531-30178-8.

PICTURE BOOK (PRIMARY THROUGH HIGH SCHOOL)

SUMMARY: Quentin Blake's zany sense of humor appeals to people of all ages, many of whom know him as the illustrator of Roald Dahl's books (including *The BFG, Matilda, The Witches, The Twits,* and others). The illustrations are hilarious, but Blake's text is equally delightful. This is an excellent book for teaching patterns in narrative. Roughly, the book follows this pattern: *Things were peaceful, but dull . . . Then came a big surprise . . . Suddenly, things grew stormy . . . Then worse . . . But finally . . . And what a relief it was!* It's a clear, easy-to-follow pattern that's a spin-off of the old set up a problem and solve it model. This one has its own special qualities, though: One is the way Zagazoo sees himself (and how his "parents" see him as he goes through some intriguing mood changes that manifest themselves physically); the other is perfectly *wonderful* dialogue—good enough to discuss and to mimic.

LESSON IDEA: Students can imitate the pattern of the story, and this is one very important and valuable way to use the book. Do not miss opportunities to focus on the dialogue, though, as well. If you wish to take some extra time, ask your students (1) why Blake uses dialogue so sparingly, and (2) what makes his dialogue work? You may wish to have them focus on dialogue for one writing assignment, with these parameters: (1) The dialogue must help the forward momentum of the story, and (2) the dialogue must be used *sparingly*—in other words, characters cannot talk about *everything,* but must speak only when it's important and they have something vital to say.

Brooks, Bruce, ed. *The Red Wasteland: A Personal Selection of Writings About Nature for Young Readers*. New York: Henry Holt and Company. 1998. ISBN: 0-8050-4495-7.

NONFICTION CHAPTER BOOK ON NATURAL SCIENCE (ELEMENTARY THROUGH HIGH SCHOOL)

SUMMARY: Many passages can be used to illustrate outstanding voice in nonfiction writing. Brooks has selected some excellent examples. *Do* read ahead, though. The chapter on hyenas, for example, is very intense, and will disturb some students. For a wonderful lesson on organization, consider Thoedore Roethke's "The Bat," the centerpiece of Chapter 2. Read Brooks' introduction, then the poem itself. He is right: The ending is a knockout.

LESSON IDEA: Have students look for fiction or nonfiction examples (poems too) in which the ending is jarring or surprising. Talk about the significance of a powerful ending.

Caney, Steven. *Steven Caney's Invention Book.* **1985. New York: Workman Publishing.** ISBN: **0-89480-076-0.**

SHORT NONFICTION ESSAYS (ELEMENTARY THROUGH HIGH SCHOOL)

SUMMARY: This book is a treasure trove of organizational examples. Caney is a master at organizing informational writing visually, chronologically, by theme, in steps, and in a variety of other ways you'll enjoy exploring. The topics are well chosen and entertaining: explore the invention of countless products from life savers to trampolines, toothpaste to cornflakes.

LESSON IDEA: Ask students to choose an invention that is *not* in Caney's book. You'll have to hunt a bit! Then, using one of his many approaches to organization, students can do ONE of the following:

- Describe the invention
- Tell its history
- Explain how to use it
- Do a diagram of the components
- Write a proposal for improving it
- Do an "interview" (fictionalized, of course) with the inventor
- Write a critique of how handy—or unhandy—this invention is!

Collard, Sneed B. III. *Sea Snakes.* **1993. Honesdale, PA: Boyds Mills Press.** ISBN: **1-56397-690-0.**

NONFICTION (PRIMARY THROUGH HIGH SCHOOL.)

SUMMARY: In this excellent informational book, Collard's many fascinating tidbits about sea snakes are so well organized that the text slips effortlessly from page to page. Yet, each "section" can be viewed as a complete essay in its own right. You can read several aloud, and identify the thread of organization by asking students, "What is the main point the author is making here?"

LESSON IDEA: With older students, go through the entire book this way, listing themes as you go, then asking them to look for an overall pattern within the themes. With younger students, take one section (essay)—try the one on page 7—and divide it into individual sentences. Cut them apart and mix them up. Then see if students can put them in order. This is an excellent group activity that asks students to think about leads, conclusions, sequencing, and transitions: the keys to good organization. Note: Students' final patterns may not match the author's original completely, and that's OK, *if* they can justify their organization. The main goal here is that it makes sense.

Dahl, Roald. *The Great Automatic Grammatizator and Other Stories*. 1997. Great Britain: Puffin Books. ISBN: 0-14-037915-0.

SHORT STORY COLLECTION (MIDDLE SCHOOL, HIGH SCHOOL)

SUMMARY: Readers familiar with Dahl's enormously popular children's stories (*Matilda, The BFG, James and the Giant Peach*) may be surprised to learn that in the 50s Dahl enjoyed a wide following as a gifted short story writer. This collection, many of them written originally for adults, has been assembled especially to appeal to a teenage audience. The stories range from humorous to subtle and even macabre, but they have one thing in common: each is a masterpiece of storytelling.

LESSON IDEA: It has been said that the best stories have turning points, much like circuitous roadways; this makes the reading all the more exciting, for just as you think you're headed in one direction, the story takes an unexpected twist. You can use this characteristic to advantage in teaching the trait of organization. Indeed, one important component of organization is direction, along with the capability of switching direction smoothly. Choose a story—I recommend "Man From the South," "The Umbrella Man," or "The Great Automatic Grammatizator"—and ask students, individually or in pairs, to identify the turning points, those places where the story takes a twist. Discuss these as a class to see how much agreement you get. This discussion can help clarify in students' minds the whole concept of "turning point." **Follow-up:** Ask students to attempt a brief short story, from 3 to 5 pages, and to think during their planning of what the turning points might be.

Fleischman, Paul. *Seedfolks*. New York: HarperCollins Publishers. 1997. ISBN: 0-06-027471-9.

CHAPTER BOOK (ELEMENTARY THROUGH HIGH SCHOOL.)

SUMMARY: Picture organization as a wheel. The hub of the wheel is the core, the central idea. Every spoke, every idea within the piece, must connect to that hub somehow. In this piece it does. Here we have

13 chapters representing 13 different voices in the inner city section of Cleveland. Each *so* individual, so different from the others. What links them together? A city garden on an old, abandoned lot (the hub of the wheel), home to refrigerators, used furniture and other throw-away items. This garden becomes the center of Fleischman's wonderfully rich and voicy little book, growing right along with the hopes and imaginings of its 13 tenants. You will also delight in the variation among the 13 voices. (A great book for teaching the trait of voice, too.) How does Fleischman *do* it? He literally becomes a different character—different

in age, sex, culture—in every chapter. Read one chapter at a time, asking students to consider questions like these: What kind of *voice* is this? Who *is* this person?

LESSON IDEA: Follow up with a similar structure in which the "hub of the wheel" is the school, the community, a group of students within the community, any organization. Ask individual students, through interviews, to create the characters (real or biographical) who make up the spokes of the wheel. They can write from their own perspectives if they prefer. The main point is to capture the voice of each character, and to show how they are related.

See also

Students who enjoy this book must not miss Fleishman's similarly organized masterwork, *Whirligig,* 1998, New York: Henry Holt and Company, Inc., ISBN: 0-8050-5582-7. (Short novel for young adults.)

Fleischman, Paul. *Weslandia.* Illustrated by Kevin Hawkes. 1999. Cambridge, MA: Candlewick Press. ISBN: 0-7636-0006-7.

PICTURE BOOK (ELEMENTARY, MIDDLE SCHOOL.)

SUMMARY: Fleischman is the master of taking one main idea and allowing it to become the center of all he writes. This is a skill worth studying, and it's ably demonstrated in *Weslandia,* the captivating story of misfit Wesley who has more tormentors than friends. He doesn't like soda or pizza, won't cut his hair in the fashion of the day, and finds the neighborhood, with its cookie cutter style houses, unbearably dreary. So, he founds his own civilization, and the rest really *is* history, history of Wesley's own making.

LESSON IDEA: Read the book aloud, more than once if you like, to give students an opportunity to make their own record of the most important events that occur. Ask them to try to see the world through Wesley's eyes as they do this. On the inside covers of the book, you'll find reproduced Wesley's history of Weslandia, written, as you'll recall once you've read the story, with his own ink (made of plant oil and soot). Invite students to create a Weslandia in your own classroom, complete with clothing, furniture, food, dishes, etc. You may also wish to chronicle Wesley's thoughts as he built his Weslandia; invite each student to do one page of Wesley's journal.

Goss, Linda and Clay. *It's Kwanzaa Time!* **1995. New York: Penguin Putnam.** ISBN: **0-399-22505-6.**

CELEBRATIONAL COLLECTION OF STORIES, TRADITIONS, AND RECIPES FOR KWANZAA (PRIMARY THROUGH HIGH SCHOOL.)

SUMMARY: Kwanzaa, an African American holiday celebrated from December 26 through January 1, is a time of great joy and family tradition. This book, filled with magnificent pictures by award- winning artists, brings us all into the festivities with its color and passion. It's organized by the seven days of the festival, and a story for each day, from "The Seven Children" to "Keep the Faith, Baby!" At the end of the book are songs, recipes, games, ideas for clothes to make and wear—even directions for creating Kwanzaa greeting cards.

LESSON IDEA: Of course you'll want to share the stories. And because there's one for each day, you can talk about the built-in organizational structure. You can also talk about what each story means, and how it adds to your understanding of what Kwanzaa is about. Ask if anyone in the class has a holiday or other tradition that is broken into parts; are birthday celebrations, for instance, sometimes organized into steps? Even games and recipes themselves are organized in a special way. As a follow-up, you may wish to pursue some of the games or recipes at the end of the book, or have students create their own greeting cards, following the ideas on page 58 of the book.

Kramer, Stephen. *Avalanche.* **Photographs by Patrick Cone. 1992. Minneapolis: Carolrhoda Books, Inc.** ISBN: **0-87614-422-9.**

INFORMATIONAL CHAPTER BOOK WITH PHOTOGRAPHIC JOURNALISM (ELEMENTARY THROUGH HIGH SCHOOL)

SUMMARY: When it comes to organizing informational writing well, Stephen Kramer is hard to top. When he does workshops for students, he brings with him the two-foot-high stack of research material it takes to come up with a half-inch thick book. As he explains to students, you cannot tell everything! You must whittle down, you must choose, you must *organize!* One of his writer's tricks, and it shows in his work, is to anticipate and answer readers' questions: Where do avalanches happen? What causes avalanches? How do you prevent avalanches, or control them? What do you do if you're caught in an avalanche? The answer(s) to each question can form the basis for a paragraph, or in this case, a chapter.

LESSON IDEA: Organize a brief research project by asking students to brainstorm, in groups, prior to any research, the questions their audience would most likely want answered. Notice that to do this well, you must know two things: (1) Who is my audience? And (2) What do they know already? This is important: you don't want to bore them with the obvious! In groups, students should answer these questions before beginning their research or even trying to come up with their list of research-guiding questions. Then, ask them to come up with NO MORE THAN SIX good questions to guide their investigations. Divide the questions up within groups, having various members work on various sections. At the end, appoint one or two copy editors (members of the group) to go through the whole document to smooth things out so it won't sound as if it's written by a committee. Great practice in group writing (a good work place skill), and excellent for developing ability to organize (and limit) information.

Organization
45

See also

- Kramer, Stephen. *Caves.* 1995. Minneapolis: Carolrhoda Books. ISBN: 0-87614-447-4.

- Kramer, Stephen. *Eye of the Storm: Chasing Storms with Warren Faidley.* 1997. New York: G.P. Putnam and Sons. ISBN: 0-399-23029-7.

- Kramer, Stephen. *Tornado.* 1992. Minneapolis: Carolrhoda Books. ISBN: 0-87614-660-4.

Patent, Dorothy Hinshaw. *Flashy Fantastic Rain Forest Frogs.* Illustrated by Kenddhl J. Jubb. 1997. New York: Walker and Company. ISBN: 0-8027-8616-2.

NONFICTION PICTURE BOOK (ELEMENTARY, MIDDLE SCHOOL.)

SUMMARY: This book is a stellar example of excellent layout. You can easily use it as a model of how to combine illustrations with text for maximum eye-catching appeal. Through Patent's easy flowing text, you'll learn much of the life of rain forest frogs, including the fact that some can be as tiny as your thumb, while others are the size of kittens! The book is also extraordinarily well-organized, and each section, which is a complete mini-essay in itself, has strong transitions that make it simple to see how one idea connects to another. It's part of what makes reading this book aloud such a pleasure.

LESSON IDEA: You might share one essay (one page) with students in hard copy or on the overhead and ask them to identify the transitional words and phrases that bind Patent's text together so neatly.

Paulsen, Gary. *My Life in Dog Years.* **1998. New York: Delacorte Press.** ISBN: **0-385-32570-3.**

BIOGRAPHICAL CHAPTER BOOK (ELEMENTARY THROUGH HIGH SCHOOL)

**Organization
46**

SUMMARY: What an intriguing way to organize your life story: by the dogs you've owned or loved! It's a simple organizational structure, but like so many simple things, works beautifully. Each chapter is named after the dog in question. The stories are lively, varied and full of voice, and great read-alouds (like all of Paulsen's work). A must for dog lovers.

LESSON IDEA: Talk about other elements that could be "organizers" for a biography: places you've lived, friends, toys owned and discarded (or saved), things collected, automobiles owned—whatever. See if students can come up with structures for potential autobiographies of their own lives. Then, they might write one chapter, a sample to give the publisher the "flavor" of the book.

Peck, Richard. *A Long Way from Chicago.* **1998. New York: Penguin Putnam.** ISBN: **0-8037-2290-7.**

CHAPTER BOOK (MIDDLE SCHOOL.)

SUMMARY: City slickers Joey and Mary Alice make an annual trek to visit Grandma Dowdel in a small Illinois town, a big change from bustling Chicago. As it turns out, though, where *Grandma* lives is where the action is. To heck with Chicago. Through a series of seven increasingly humorous trips, Joey and Mary Alice grow and change, in their perspective and their knowledge of the world.

LESSON IDEA: Time is a common organizer in writing, but not every author takes advantage of it as Peck does here. As you read and share the story, keep track of the changes you and your students see in the main characters and the way they see the world. How much time must go by before a character can see the world with a "new vision"? For writers who feel ready, try a piece in which a fair amount of time lapses. Share the main character's perspective at one point in time, then at another, down the road a year (or whatever feels right to make the "vision" change). One example might be looking at the gym of your elementary school the day you leave to go on—then returning a year or two later and walking into that same gym. What has changed? You or the gym? Or both?

Sachar, Louis. *Holes*. New York: Farrar, Straus and Giroux. 1998. ISBN: 0-374-33265-7.

YOUNG ADULT NOVEL (MIDDLE SCHOOL, HIGH SCHOOL)

SUMMARY: Camp Green Lake is not the typical camp. But in the very beginning of the book, we do not really know why. We get hints, though. The ominous-sounding warden. The deadly lizards. And of course, the holes. *Why* do the campers dig holes? What sort of camp *is* this? Sachar's book keeps you guessing and wanting more. One of the greatest read-aloud books ever.

LESSON IDEA: Think how often we describe good organization as having a beginning, middle, and end. Students eventually figure out what we mean by a beginning and an end, but what the heck is the *middle*? Maybe it's the detailed answers to all those questions raised by the beginning. Begin by reading just the first chapter aloud; it's only two pages. Then, brainstorm a list of questions that pop into your mind when you hear this haunting lead. Predict some answers to the questions. *Hang on to this list.* As you read on and the questions are answered, compare your predictions to what really happens. See how close you come.

Extension: Next time students write, fiction or nonfiction, ask them to make a list of questions that might pop up in the minds of a reader. It is good to do this with a partner, so you have someone to check your thinking. Anticipating, predicting, and following through by answering questions are all excellent organizational skills.

Snedden, Robert. *YUCK! A Big Book of Little Horrors*. 1996. New York: Simon and Schuster. ISBN: 0-689-80676-0.

ILLUSTRATED CHAPTER BOOK ON SCIENCE (ELEMENTARY THROUGH HIGH SCHOOL)

SUMMARY: You need to see this book to appreciate it. First, the illustrations—magnified thousands of times—are fascinating. But second, the book's layout is an artistic lesson in how to build suspense into nonfiction writing. You see the magnified illustration of, say, a dust mite. You might know immediately what it is, but perhaps your students will not, and believe me, they'll enjoy guessing. Then you can read a few leading lines that give you hints about what you're looking at. Now, unfold the flap, peek inside, and get the *rest* of the story. Very imaginative layout this is!

LESSON IDEA: Next time you do a research piece, follow the format. You'll need 11 × 14 sheets of paper to do this (one per student). Holding each paper horizontally, create a flap by folding over, from the right, a piece equal to about one third the 14" length of the sheet. As you face the paper, the folded flap should be *on the right.* The left single-sheet side of the paper is for the illustration. The right *outside* panel is for the opening text (the lead), and the inside (the part that doesn't show till you open the flap) is for the main body of the text, which will contain your "punchline" information. This format encourages students to save the best for last, and also to put a few intriguing "teasers" right up front.

Steig, William. *Amos and Boris.* **1971. New York: Farrar, Straus and Giroux. ISBN: 0-374-30278-2.**

VIC'S PICKS

PICTURE BOOK (PRIMARY THROUGH HIGH SCHOOL)

SUMMARY: William Steig is the king of wordsmithery, and this book is his masterpiece. It is a verbal symphony, and also a superb example of fine plotting. Use it for word choice, certainly, but also to teach the concept of narrative writing: not just a list of unrelated events, but closely interwoven, purposeful happenings that all relate and all lead to some revelation or larger truth. All good stories have turning points (sometimes easier to see looking at a film or TV show). Read the book and ask students to identify the *most important* moments. What's significant here? (Hint: Boris saves Amos's life; Amos saves Boris's life. These are BIG events compared to, say, building the boat. But students do not always see the difference.)

LESSON IDEA: Chart *Amos and Boris.* Draw a horizontal line graph that rises during action sequences and falls during more quiet periods. You can do this as a class activity, or ask students to do it in groups. This activity teaches two important concepts of narrative writing: (1) nothing happens without a reason, and (2) good narratives rise and fall like mountains or waves, with peak periods of action (and, usually, one or two *standout* high points). Follow up by asking students to write a short narrative, then graph it in the same way, showing the high's and low's. This can be *very* revealing! (What if you don't *have* any high's and low's? Maybe you don't really *have* a story line! Oops . . .) By the way, don't hesitate to use this book with high schoolers. Both theme and plot, deceptively simple, have great depth, and the graphing is a challenge.

Thorne-Thomsen, Kathleen. *Frank Lloyd Wright for Kids.* **1994. Chicago: Chicago Review Press. ISBN: 1-55652-207-X.**

NONFICTION BIOGRAPHY/INFORMATIONAL CHAPTER BOOK (ELEMENTARY, MIDDLE SCHOOL.)

SUMMARY: Fascinating and beautifully illustrated, this book takes students into the world of architect Frank Lloyd Wright. The book itself is a masterpiece of organization, moving from details about Lloyd Wright's life and family to his extraordinary ability to perceive patterns and visual images in the nature around them, and then transform those patterns into buildings that have enchanted the world. The book includes a wide range of activities that allow students to use their own imaginations to read architectural plans, build simple models, design a city—even copy some of Frank's favorite recipes.

LESSON IDEA: Lessons are built in since the book is packed with activities. If you want to do something more, you might analyze the organization of the book itself, noticing both how chapters are laid out and how information, chapter to chapter, is integrated. How is this smooth design a tribute to Frank Lloyd Wright himself?

Weber, Ken. *Five-Minute Mysteries: 37 Challenging Cases of Murder and Mayhem for You to Solve.* **1989. Philadelphia: Running Press.** ISBN: **0-89471-690-5.**

UNSOLVED SHORT MYSTERIES (MIDDLE SCHOOL, HIGH SCHOOL)

SUMMARY: Are you a good listener? Perceptive? Good at spotting clues? Test your skills at reconstructing a crime or identifying the perpetrator with 37 short (2–3 pages) mysteries, each with clues carefully embedded. You only have to pay attention!

LESSON IDEA: Read various stories aloud. You may wish to pick and choose. Then invite students to discuss the stories in groups to see who can solve them. As a follow-up, invite students to write mysteries of their own, with hidden clues, of course, and invite others in the class to solve them. Have fun with this one! It's a painless way to learn that in good fiction of any kind, not only mysteries, every detail serves a purpose, and points to an ending that seems inevitable once you know it.

Wiesner, David. *Sector 7.* **1999. New York: Houghton Mifflin.** ISBN: **0-395-74656-6.**

VIC'S PICKS

WORDLESS PICTURE BOOK (PRIMARY THROUGH HIGH SCHOOL.)

SUMMARY: This story of an extraordinary visit to the observatory is alive with detail, highly amusing, filled with personality clashes and adventures, and enriched with incredibly imaginary dialogue. Only *none* of it is written down. It's all contained within the artistry of David Wiesner, who knows how to pack a picture with meaning, then string a whole series of pictures together to let us tell our own versions.

LESSON IDEA: Take time to look closely at the pictures; if you skim through, you'll miss worlds of meaning. Wiesner fills *every corner* with detail, so you *do* need to pay attention. (This is an outstanding book for building observation skills.) Younger readers may wish the first time through to simply focus on what is happening in each picture, and how the story is changing as they go. Ask them to explain it orally to you; don't be the interpreter, tempting though that is. Older reader/writers can do the same as a base for creating their own interpretive stories. Important questions to answer as you go: Does everyone see what the boy in the story sees? Why is he singled out for this madcap adventure? How do the managers of the observatory feel about the whole thing? How do you know? How does Wiesner get meaning across without words? (List as many ways that he does this as you can think of.) **Extension:** What happens next? Invite older writers to extend the tale through text or pictures or both. You may also wish to have a discussion on the value of wordless picture books: How do they stretch a reader's imagination?

Wysocki, Charles. *Heartland.* **1994. New York: Artisan.**
ISBN: **1-885183-05-4.**

JOURNAL, MEMOIR, ART COLLECTION (PRIMARY THROUGH HIGH SCHOOL)

SUMMARY: In this incredibly appealing book, American legend and folk artist Charles Wyswocki combines his eloquent thoughts—"There is a country in my mind, a landscape in my heart, a place that does not appear on any map but is so clear and sharply detailed that to paint it, I have only to look within" (Introduction)—with sketches, snapshots, and of course, his highly original paintings.

LESSON IDEA: Wysocki organizes his information around the major themes that have influenced his thinking as an artist: *Through the Eyes of a Child, The Bounty of the Earth, The Charm of America, The Worth of Work, The Lure of the Sea,* and *The Joy of Love.* Teach this to students by having them think through the themes of their own lives. Ask, "What is most important to you if you had to break it down into just five topics?" This is a tough question, so expect some need for time, and some need to work in pairs or teams. Then you can ask the same question—What are the major themes?—related to *any* topic, from good driving habits to manners to wetlands to the Civil War. This kind of "chunking" is an excellent organizational tool. Don't feel compelled to follow up the organizational thinking with actual writing. Just keep practicing the "chunking" till thinking in themes becomes comfortable. Then, go back and look at Wysocki's work again. Ask why he organized it this way, rather than, say, chronologically. Which structure works better? Which tells more?

Books for Teaching
Voice

Favorite books always have voice; that's why they become favorites! But what exactly is this elusive trait so many writers and readers have tried to define? To judge by the diversity in this collection, voice is many things: confidence, enthusiasm, personality, individual expressiveness, a desire to reach out to the reader through language, a way of revealing a writer's feelings or attitudes toward a subject, or, as one teacher put it, "the writer's fingerprints on the page." The voices in these books are as varied as the writers themselves. Some are humorous or whimsical, some serious or reflective. Together, they provide a collection that can help show students how diverse voice can be—and what a strong tool voice is (whether in a mystery story or an expository essay) for influencing readers and for gaining and holding their attention.

Teach voice by

- Reading aloud
- Writing letters
- Identifying the "best" voice for an audience
- Describing and comparing voices
- Responding to art

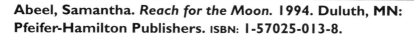

Abeel, Samantha. *Reach for the Moon.* **1994. Duluth, MN: Pfeifer-Hamilton Publishers. ISBN: 1-57025-013-8.**

REFLECTIONS ON WORKS OF ART (ELEMENTARY THROUGH HIGH SCHOOL)

Voice
52

SUMMARY: Are you wearing a watch? Near a clock? Look at it now. Imagine having such a struggle with math that you cannot tell time. What you see on the face of the clock or watch has no meaning for you. That was Samantha's story, and it left her feeling like a failure, hating seventh grade. Then, with the help of an intuitive and supportive teacher, she found her voice—in writing. Samantha writes in response to the beautiful watercolor paintings of Charles Murphy: ". . . if you're standing in the shadow of the tree, you may need to walk to the other side to see the light it reflects . . . This is my reflection of the light. Welcome to my book." Samantha was 13 when she told her story. It will steal your heart.

LESSON IDEA: Read the introduction written by Samantha aloud—and other selected pieces, too. Asking students to write about one personal difficulty overcome (as Samantha does in her introduction to the book) is an obvious offshoot, and it's one possibility. To make more profound use of this lesson, give students an opportunity to respond to art. Check out Samantha's poems "Quilt" and "Leaves in the Fall" to see the powerful influence of art on thinking. Give students time to explore the world of art, and to choose *one* piece that "speaks" to them, then to respond in any form, be it a journal entry, letter, poem, personal essay, critique, or story.

Albom, Mitch. *Tuesdays With Morrie.* **1997. New York: Bantam, Doubleday, Dell Publishing. ISBN: 0-385-48451-8.**

VIC'S PICKS

BIOGRAPHICAL NOVEL (HIGH SCHOOL)

SUMMARY: Morrie Schwartz is dying. The reason Mitch Albom cares about this so much is that Morrie was his favorite teacher, the one he promised he'd return to visit. Return he does, just in time, to learn the lessons of life, death, and how to make it through. It's a story, yes, but mostly it's a book of philosophy, one you will not want to put down. Read it aloud if you can. It's an emotional roller coaster, but the laughs keep you going through the rest.

LESSON IDEA: Ask students to create their own philosophical commentary. As they listen to the book, collect (you'll need to write them down) comments, thoughts, ideas, reflections that catch someone's attention from your class. By the end of this short book, you should have quite a list. Print it up, and ask students to use one or two of the comments as a springboard for their own philosophical thoughts on life, death, and all that happens in between. Consider creating a class book of personal essays and reflections.

Barry, Dave. *Dave Barry in Cyberspace.* **1997. New York: Fawcett Books.** ISBN: **0-449-91230-2.**

SATIRICAL COLLECTION OF ESSAYS ON COMPUTERS (HIGH SCHOOL)

SUMMARY: Anyone who's ever wrestled with a surly computer will find a laugh or two in this book detailing the joys and pains of the computer age. It's an excellent book for teaching satirical tone: how to use it for comic effect, controlling the tone so you don't go over the edge (you can overdo exaggeration if you make things a billion times worse than they really are), and speaking to your audience.

LESSON IDEA: Read a passage or two aloud and ask students to rate each for voice. As an alternative, you might invite students to select a passage to use as the basis of a lesson *they* construct and present on voice, focusing on humor and audience connection. You may also wish to compare a passage from Barry's book to one from a serious manual on using computers. Ask these questions: How do the voices compare? Why do they differ? How does voice connect to purpose? How does voice influence meaning?

Bauer, Marion Dane. *On My Honor.* **1986. New York: Houghton Mifflin.** ISBN: **0-89919-439-7.**

YOUNG ADULT NOVEL (MIDDLE SCHOOL)

SUMMARY: What is guilt all about? How responsible are we for the lives of others? And what if a decision results in a tragedy that cannot be undone, that cannot be remedied? These are questions that haunt us as we go from adolescence to adulthood. They're especially haunting for Joel, who fears he may be responsible for the death of his good friend Tony. How does a person live with so much moral weight upon his shoulders? Find out as you share a short but riveting story that does not take the easy way out.

LESSON IDEA: This book raises intriguing but difficult moral questions, many of which would make good subjects for persuasive writing. For example, at the close of the story, Joel feels a huge sense of responsibility for what occurred. Should he? Here's another: When you promise *on your honor* that you will or will not do something, how much weight should those words carry? Is there *ever* an exception? If so, explain when or why that might occur.

Bloor, Edward. *Tangerine*. 1997. New York: Scholastic. ISBN: 0-590-43277-X.

YOUNG ADULT NOVEL (MIDDLE SCHOOL, HIGH SCHOOL)

SUMMARY: A remarkable page turner that takes a realistic look at sibling rivalry and resentment as well as race relations and class snobbery. Paul Fisher is a most unusual hero. He wears thick glasses, has trouble fitting in, and is virtually ignored by his family. When forced to move to Tangerine, Florida, Paul tries hard to make the best of things, and winds up not only learning a lot about how real friendship works, but also teaching others about living up to your own definition of morality.

LESSON IDEA: This book simply vibrates with voice. But instead of tracking down the voice-filled passages yourself, ask students to do it. Make a bulletin board collection of their findings, or, have some students read them aloud. **Alternative:** Ask students to imagine they are journalists interviewing Paul, his father, mother, brother Erik, Tino, or any other major character within the story. Post the results so students can see how their classmate "read" the characters within the book. Notice how much strong characters contribute to voice in fiction writing.

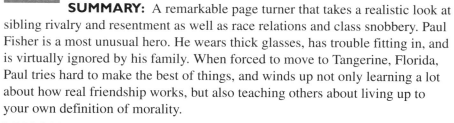

Branzei, Sylvia. *Grossology Begins At Home: The Science of Really Gross Things in Your Everyday Life*. 1997. New York: Addison Wesley Longman. ISBN: 0-201-95993-3.

NONFICTION CHAPTER BOOK ON SCIENCE (ELEMENTARY, MIDDLE SCHOOL)

SUMMARY: Did you know that a medium sized chocolate bar can contain up to 90 insect fragments and three rodent hairs (p. 62)? Or that a one-pound bag of popcorn might contain two rodent hairs, while an 8-ounce can of cocoa powder could contain 18 rodent hairs and up to 562 (ye gods) insect fragments? (p. 65) Frozen Brussels sprouts often contain dozens of aphids, but who cares? Who eats *those*? (p. 65) These and hundreds of other "gross" factoids fill Branzei's very funny, informative, and—let's be honest—some would say, very offensive book. The language tends toward the vulgar in spots. I know many people will say, "Oh, lighten up—that's the way kids themselves talk!" Exactly. Branzei has transformed science into kid talk, and *they do* find it intriguing and hard to put down. They learn a lot, too. This is a well-researched book. Use it to illustrate expository writing with voice, *and* the importance of digging for that detail (aphids!) that makes your readers sit up and smell the Brussels sprouts.

LESSON IDEA: Dig for what Barry Lane calls the "potatoes"—the interesting facts under the surface. Give students a list of no more than six potential topics to choose from. Use one of Branzei's books as a starting point if you wish, but any topics will do. Have them work in teams of two to four to dig up the six most interesting facts they can on the ONE subject of each team's choice. Write a short paragraph incorporating all intriguing facts, and read aloud to the class. Tip: Students do NOT have to go for shock value, but their details MUST be interesting. No common knowledge allowed.

See also

- Branzei, Sylvia. *Animal Grossology.* 1996. New York: Addison Wesley Longman. ISBN: 0-201-95994-1.
- Branzei, Sylvia. *Grossology: The Science of Really Gross Things!* 1995. New York: Addison Wesley Longman. ISBN: 0-201-40964-X

Brooks, Bruce. *Predator!* 1991. New York: Farrar, Straus and Giroux. ISBN: 0-374-36112-6.

VIC'S PICKS NONFICTION CHAPTER BOOK (ELEMENTARY THROUGH HIGH SCHOOL)

SUMMARY: Cover to cover, one of the finest examples of expository writing with voice you can find. Open it to *any* chapter and find excellent read-aloud examples. Caution, though: If you're the squeamish type, this might not be your book. Students *love* it—every class I've ever shared it with has. But it is honest, graphic and to the point about its theme: Many animals must kill to survive. That includes us: "In truth, human beings are pretty wimpy predators. Very few hunt all the meat they eat, unless you call looking at newspaper ads to find which store has the cheapest chuck steak a hunt" (p. 57).

LESSON IDEA: Compare Brooks' science-as-drama approach to the information provided in, say, an encyclopedia or textbook. Why is one written with so much more voice? What effect does this have on audience, and when is voice within informational writing most appropriate? **Extension:** How much does the author's knowledge of his/her subject influence voice? Want to find out? Ask students to write 200 words on any animal about which they know *nothing.* Now, have them spend one week digging up all the information on that creature they can. Write 400 words this time. Compare the two for voice *and* detail.

Curry, Boykin and Brian Kasbar, editors. *Essays That Worked: 50 Essays from Successful Applications to the Nation's Top Colleges.* **1990. New York: Random House.** ISBN: **0-449-90517-9.**

COLLECTION OF STUDENTS' COLLEGE APPLICATION ESSAYS
(MIDDLE SCHOOL, HIGH SCHOOL)

Voice 56

SUMMARY: High school teachers in particular will *not* want to be without this book. Though not all college-bound students must write application essays, many will, and essay writing is a useful skill for building a sense of focus, organization, and voice. One thing *all* these essays have in common is voice, and the authors make it quite clear that this trait is essential to their success. Best of all, though, the voices are not all alike; some are whimsical, some poignant, some serious and dignified, some outrageous. Diversity is the order of the day.

LESSON IDEA: Read an essay every 2 to 3 days or one per week, whatever you have time for. Talk about the kinds of voices you hear. See how many words students can come up with to describe each voice. **Extension:** Ask students to write their own essays, answering questions like these (or come up with questions of your own):

• Who has been your best teacher? Why?

• What author, if any, do you feel no reader should miss?

• What are the three most important things a person gets out of a good education?

• In earlier times, many persons were said to be self-educated. Will this still be possible in the twenty-first century?

• What is the single greatest threat to the survival of the human race?

• What is the single most important thing a person could learn about you?

See also (for a slightly more technical spin on the same theme):

• Curry, Boykin, editor. *Essays That Worked for Law Schools.* 1991. New York: Random House. ISBN: 0-449-90515-2.

• Curry, Boykin and Brian Kasbar, editors. *Essays That Worked for Business Schools.* 1991. New York: Random House. ISBN: 0-449-90516-0.

Dahl, Roald. *The Twits.* **Illustrated by Quentin Blake. 1981. New York: Puffin Books.** ISBN: **0-14-130107-4.**

ILLUSTRATED CHAPTER BOOK (PRIMARY THROUGH HIGH SCHOOL)

SUMMARY: It's foul. It's obnoxious. It's disgusting. It's—it's *The Twits!* A favorite with students—*and* adults—of all ages. The lesson of this book (beyond humor, of course) is that abject honesty augments voice. Dahl looks life right in the eye.

LESSON IDEA: Honesty is *one* key to voice. Ask students to write an exceptionally honest piece about something that they find annoying, disgusting, provoking, scary, or irritating. If they do not wish to share these pieces aloud, they make fine journal entries, but encourage sharing from anyone who's willing because hearing the results is an important part of this lesson. Talk about the "risk-taking" aspect of voice that comes from total honesty.

Ehrlich, Amy, ed. *When I Was Your Age.* 1996. Cambridge, MA: Candlewick Press. ISBN: 1-56402-306-0.

AUTOBIOGRAPHICAL SKETCHES (ELEMENTARY THROUGH HIGH SCHOOL)

SUMMARY: This is a book of memories: theirs (the autobiographical recollections of 10 well-known writers), and *yours*. For you will identify, and it will take you back. This is the power of this wonderful read-aloud book. You needn't read them all (though you may want to). Katherine Patterson's "Why I Never Ran Away From Home" is written with such expression you cannot help but read it with voice.

LESSON IDEA: Memories make for great narratives. Why not attach them to photographs as the authors in this book do? After reading two, three or more of the selections from this book, have students select a favorite or (much more fun) *least* favorite photo and write the story behind it. Make a class book or share them.

Feelings, Tom. *The Middle Passage.* 1995. New York: Dial Books. ISBN: 0-8037-1804-7.

WORDLESS STORY TOLD THROUGH ART (MIDDLE SCHOOL, HIGH SCHOOL)

SUMMARY: This is more than a book. It's an achievement. Dare to look closely at the detail in these startling, hair-raising pictures and you will see images of horror and hope. Courage and despair. Turn the pages and trace a journey of agony, one that only the strongest will survive. Tom Feelings' vivid, passionate sketches portray the amazing resilience of those who traveled the slave ships to America packed like chord wood. The lesson here is that pictures, like text, have voice. Take a look. Feel the chill.

LESSON IDEA: Students might imagine themselves in the role of one of Feelings' characters, then create a journal entry or series of entries to reflect that individual's voice through his/her experience. Why would anyone choose to jump off the ship to certain death rather than complete the journey? What is in the mind of such a courageous person on the night before jumping among the sharks? **Alternative:** Ask students to look for other pictures that reflect voice (voice of any kind; it need not echo the voice of Feelings' book). Then see how close they can come to describing the voice in those pictures.

Fiffer, Sharon Sloan and Steve Fiffer, eds. *Home*. 1995. New York: Random House. ISBN: 0-679-44206-5.

MEMOIRS (MIDDLE SCHOOL, HIGH SCHOOL)

SUMMARY: In this extraordinary collection, eighteen writers share their recollections of "home," whatever that might mean to them. For many, it's a special corner that holds indelible memories. For some, it's a feeling, a time, an atmosphere. And it's interesting to note how they all seem to choose slightly different locations, different voices and moods to bring the memories alive. Some are hilarious, some poignant. All have heart.

LESSON IDEA: This book is an excellent introduction to a unit on *place* as a theme. What are your roots? What is your sense of place, and how did it shape who you are and how you think? Read several chapters aloud, then give students time to jot down impressions and record memories of their own; time to talk in small groups may be helpful, too. Once you've read four or five entries, let students write their own home theme pieces and share in groups. Great for developing detail and personal voice.

Fleischman, Paul. *Bull Run*. 1993. New York: HarperCollins Publishers. ISBN: 0-06-440588-5.

HISTORY-BASED NOVEL TOLD THROUGH MULTIPLE VOICES (ELEMENTARY, MIDDLE SCHOOL)

SUMMARY: In this multi-award winning novel, Paul Fleischman "relies on individual human voices to give a human face to history" (Review by *Publishers Weekly*, reprinted in the HarperCollins edition). The book can be read or performed. Either way, you will hear about the Civil War as it is often presented on video, through the voices of those who were there: in this case, sixteen persons, black and white, male and female, from both sides of the conflict. Follow their dreams and nightmares, their passions and conflicts through brief but captivating glimpses into their thinking.

LESSON IDEA: Fleischman's approach to organization in this breathtaking novel is classic, and you can easily imitate it by assigning role-playing parts to students studying any period of history. They can invent characters or assume the identity of actual historic figures, and write what they believe those persons might have thought or said. That is one way to use the book. In addition, though, do not miss the opportunity to perform readers' theater, assigning parts and allowing students to speak those parts in their own voices. For extra enrichment, invent some new characters whose voices can mix with those of Fleischman's sixteen originals. Students will be challenged trying to match the voice of this powerful writer.

Gantos, Jack. *Jack's Black Book*. 1997. New York: Farrar, Straus and Giroux. ISBN: 0-374-43716-5.

VIC'S PICKS

CHAPTER BOOK (MIDDLE SCHOOL)

Voice 59

SUMMARY: A hilarious read-aloud in which we follow the inner thoughts of Jack as he attempts to write the great American novel. Anyone who has struggled with writing or ever felt just plain left out of it will identify and laugh. A blatantly honest book that clearly illustrates the use of voice and detail in personal narrative.

LESSON IDEA: Share the book aloud, and occasionally, at the end of a chapter (or chapters, if your students won't let you quit), ask students to list favorite words, expressions, or images. Talk about how these contribute to voice. As you go along, you might also create a collection of words (zany, quirky) that describe Jack's voice. The book also makes a great lead-in to personal journal entries about feelings and responses to events.

Grutman, Jewel H. and Gay Matthaei. *Julia Singing Bear*. 1996. West Palm Beach, FL: Lickle Publishing. ISBN: 1-56566-095-1.

HISTORY-BASED FICTIONAL JOURNAL (ELEMENTARY, MIDDLE SCHOOL)

SUMMARY: Few things are better for teaching voice than journal writing. Here's a primary example: it's a fictional example created in consultation with Lakota Sioux tribal member and Lakota Studies professor Arthur Amiotte. Julia's journal tells of her early life with her people, notably her grandparents, and her later efforts (after her parents are killed) to bridge the gap between white and Native American cultures at the Carlisle Indian School. Gorgeous, authentic illustrations, many done in the style of 1800s photographs.

Exceptional sensitivity to cultural issues. Also see the magnificent companion-piece, *The Ledgerbook of Thomas Blue Eagle* (same authors, same theme, same attention to authentic detail). ISBN for *Thomas Blue Eagle:* 1-56566-063-3.

LESSON IDEA: This book is an excellent introductory piece to an extended journal writing activity in which students record the life of a historical character (or a fictional character who lived at some time in history that they may be studying). The more complete the research, the better and more authentic the journal will be. Lesson point: Really *good* fiction has research roots!

Hesse, Karen. *Out of the Dust.* **1997. New York: Scholastic Press.** ISBN: **0-590-36080-9.**

VIC'S PICKS

CHAPTER BOOK IN FREE VERSE (MIDDLE SCHOOL, HIGH SCHOOL)

Voice 60

SUMMARY: A gripping, compelling portrait of life in the Dust Bowl era, as viewed through the eyes of a 13-year-old girl. Voice is so often equated with humor that it is important to remind students that voices can be reflective, serious, soulful, passionate—or professionally businesslike. In this case, the voice is intense, fearful, courageous, determined, wistful, heartbroken, and hopeful, too. Because the text is written in free verse, you'll find you're teaching fluency, too, as you read aloud. An excellent precursor to *The Grapes of Wrath* or any study of the 1930s, the Dust Bowl, or the Depression. Also an excellent addition to any unit on poetry.

LESSON IDEA: Read just the first chapter and the magic will hook you. It's a shame not to read the whole thing aloud, especially since it isn't long. Individual chapters are *very* short, and take only a few minutes each. Ask students to describe the kind of voice they hear in each chapter. (You may wish them to be readers, too.) The voice fluctuates, but never loses power. Also discuss the fact it is written in first person, journal fashion. What difference do these things make to voice? **Extension:** You can go in many directions with a book this great as your launching point. Students may wish to write about a personal experience in free verse form. They may also wish to extend the writing by creating a companion piece from the perspective of another character. In "Out of the Dust," we hear only the girl's voice, not the father's. Some students may wish to create a short passage expressing his perspective (or that of any other character in the book).

Hill, Anthony. *The Burnt Stick.* 1995. Boston: Houghton Mifflin Company. ISBN: 0-395-73974-8.

FACT-BASED SHORT NOVEL (ELEMENTARY THROUGH HIGH SCHOOL)

SUMMARY: Warning: This is a heart wrenching story. Be prepared. Yet, it is based on truth, and is a story that needs telling. John Jagamarra lives with his mother on the far northwest coast of Australia. John is half aborigine, half white. The law says, therefore, he must be taken from his aboriginal mother, who is not really viewed as a person, and sent to live with his father in a white man's world. For a long time, the magic of the burnt stick, which colors his skin dark, works to disguise him and keep him at his mother's side. But in the end, it is the men with rules and trucks who prevail.

LESSON IDEA: Though the text of this story is simple, the lesson it tells is not, and the feelings it arouses in us are passionate. Voice is part that: the ability to move another person in order to bring greater meaning to the text. Ask students to use what they feel in composing letters that might have been sent to the Welfare Department on John Jagamarra's behalf. What argument might have helped them see the truth of what they were doing to families and to children's sense of self-worth? As your students write, ask them to keep John's mother's perspective in mind. Why do the Welfare men feel they have the right to treat her as they do?

Voice
61

Kardong, Don. *Hills, Hawgs & Ho Chi Minh: More Tales of a Wayward Runner.* 1996. Sandpoint, ID: Keokee Publishing. ISBN: 1-879628-12-0.

NONFICTION CHAPTER BOOK ON FITNESS & RUNNING (MIDDLE SCHOOL, HIGH SCHOOL)

SUMMARY: And now for something completely different. There are surely lots of books out there on fitness. But not that many on the fine, memorable moments of being a runner. Here's a tidbit: "Observing a 100-mile run, you're prepared for the struggle. You know this will be a grand sumo mismatch, where each human—steeled through months of training, myopically focused, and yet appearing small, wizened, not quite up to the task—will square off against his or her colossal opponent: a rugged, sometimes precipitous, intermittently gloomy, seemingly unending stretch of wilderness." (p. 234) Now *that's* fine writing. Full of voice, with well-chosen language that is both poetic and suited to the athletic world. The chapter on marathon runner Johnny Kelley will set you afire.

LESSON IDEA: Almost everyone has a memorable athletic experience, heroic or otherwise. Successes (homeruns and touchdowns) make for great copy, but the truth is, the best stories are often about the times it didn't all work out. After reading some passages aloud, you might ask students to write a paragraph on an athletic "happening" that did or did *not* turn out well. **Variations:** Write from more than one perspective: You and the coach. You and an opponent. Write a before and after journal entry. Write a news story in which you cover a brief "play of the day." Write an ad for a local health club that would get out-of-shape folks to join.

 Little, Jean. *Hey World, Here I Am!* 1986. New York: HarperCollins Publishers. ISBN: 0-06-440384-X.

 YOUNG ADULT COLLECTION OF ESSAYS AND POEMS (ELEMENTARY, MIDDLE SCHOOL)

SUMMARY: Sure to touch your heart, and to make you think. The language is deceptively simple, the ideas deep and thought-provoking. In Jean Little's classic book, we see the world through the eyes of young Kate Bloomfeld, who is doing her best to grow up and finding some days a whole lot harder than others. You will laugh aloud and cry, too. This is real life. No fantasies, no spaceships on which to escape. Do not miss the chapters called "Five Dollars" and "Mrs. Buell," two favorites.

LESSON IDEA: Voice often comes from real-life writing: writing that's honest and holds nothing back. This is why, in personal narrative writing, voice can be risky. As you share the book, ask students to brainstorm the qualities of real-life writing: honesty, good observation of detail, insight into the feelings of others, etc. Then, ask them to try their hands at this real-life writing, perhaps in a private journal entry first. Write a short piece yourself; a paragraph is enough. Prose or poetry. Share your piece, and invite others to do the same. **Extension:** If you have shared any segments from *SeinLanguage* (Jerry Seinfeld's book), take some time to discuss the differences in tone between the two books. How would you describe Kate's (Jean Little's) voice? How would you describe Jerry's? What makes the difference?

 Littlechild, George. *This Land Is My Land.* 1993. San Francisco, CA: Children's Book Press. ISBN: 0-89239-119-7.

 PORTFOLIO OF ART WITH REFLECTIVE WRITINGS (PRIMARY THROUGH HIGH SCHOOL)

SUMMARY: George Littlechild connects text to art in a remarkable and moving way. This book is a collection of his work, with moving and insightful reflections on each piece. Most remarkable, though, is the tone this writer achieves: powerful, yet so very restrained. You'll feel for a moment how it was to be a small Native American child at a white school receiving the red stars instead of the gold ones, knowing the red meant your work was not very good. Littlechild can break your heart like nobody's business without resorting to one *ounce* of sentimentality.

LESSON IDEA: Try achieving voice through art. Students need not be gifted painters or sculptors to make this work; a poster, photograph, or collage will work just as well as a personal piece. Then, after sharing a number of Littlechild's pieces, ask students to reflect on their work and the meaning behind it or their own personal connection to the work.

Masson, Jeffrey Moussaieff. *The Emperor's Embrace: Reflections on Animal Families and Fatherhood.* **1999. New York: Simon & Schuster. ISBN: 0-671-02083-8.**

Voice
63

ESSAYS ON NATURAL SCIENCE (MIDDLE SCHOOL, HIGH SCHOOL)

SUMMARY: Beautifully, wonderfully researched, Masson's fascinating book is both highly informative and moving. The language is impeccably clear: "It is odd how often we use wild animals to symbolize human preoccupations—bravery, war, romantic love, luck—but how rarely we actually look at the genuine characteristics of the animal" (p. 95). Masson paints irresistable portraits of loving father frogs and seahorses; nurturing, tender Emperor Penguins; caring and protective wild dogs and wolves; and their rather indifferent domesticated cousins. He also discusses dangerous animal fathers: e.g., lions and bears. Through his carefully selected examples, we get a wonderfully full, detailed portrait of fatherhood throughout the animal kingdom. An excellent example of just-right voice in informational writing, and perfect follow-up to the version for younger students: Sneed B. Collard's *Animal Dads* (see Ideas).

LESSON IDEA: Read several selected samples aloud (a paragraph to two pages or more). Talk about the *kind* of voice you hear in the writing. Brainstorm, as a class, words to describe Masson's voice. Then try this: Pass out an encyclopedia excerpt on one of the animals Masson discusses in his book (an animal you have NOT read about yet). Make your encyclopedia passage short, but fairly information-full. Ask students to re-write it, capturing a bit of Masson's reader friendly voice without sacrificing content. Talk about the kinds of changes they have made. Then, read Masson's counterpart piece; the content will be different, of course, but you can compare the voices. Were your students successful in making their writing reader-directed, easy going, and extremely clear? Does the "right" voice come through: informative and friendly, a balance of personal and factual?

Murphy, Jim. *The Boy's War: Confederate and Union Soldiers Talk About the Civil War.* 1990. New York: Houghton Mifflin. ISBN: 0-395-66412-8.

NONFICTION CHAPTER BOOK (MIDDLE SCHOOL, HIGH SCHOOL)

SUMMARY: Powerful photographs, quotations from journals and letters, and historical records combine to create a history of the Civil War that's alive and real. It is startling to realize that so many of the war's soldiers were mere boys, 12 to 14 years old.

LESSON IDEA: You might choose selected passages to read aloud, or you may find yourself coerced into doing the whole book. It does read like a novel. It's a great launching pad for research. With your students, keep a list of potential topics as you go: how boys so young got into the army in the first place, kinds of uniforms, kinds of weapons used, "training," measles, food in the camps, how mail reached the troops, and on and on. A thousand fascinating topics will present themselves as you go. Students can each choose a topic and become the resident expert on that subject. Your short research pieces can become chapters for a larger class book. Here's a provocative question your students might respond to in writing: What if 12-year-old boys were drafted into the army *today* in the U.S.? How might that change our culture or our history? Also, are there places in the world where this still happens? What are the implications for *their* culture?

O'Neal, Shaquille. *Shaq and the Beanstalk and Other Very Tall Tales.* Illustrated by Shane W. Evans. 1999. New York: Scholastic. ISBN: 0-590-91823-0.

PICTURE BOOK (ELEMENTARY THROUGH HIGH SCHOOL)

SUMMARY: What if you could walk right into a fairy tale and make yourself part of the story? That's exactly what Shaquille O'Neal does in this wild and wacky romp through the fairy tales that Shaq recalls as his personal favorites. This time around, though, they get a slight spin as the NBA star plays with both plot and character in order to weave his own way of thinking and speaking into the fairy tale traditions. It is definitely his own voice and no one else's: e.g., when the near-sighted three bears cannot find their glasses and mistake Shaq for a slightly changed Goldilocks, his comment is, "Say what? . . . Who are you calling Goldilocks?" Older readers, who know both the stories and fairy tale traditions, and who can appreciate O'Neal's playful liberties with the voices of the originals will find his renditions humorous and refreshing.

LESSON IDEA: This is a book to prompt some real fun—and exploration of students' personal voices. You can ask them to inject themselves into favorite fairy tales. Don't forget the importance of including dialogue with the characters. Haven't you always wanted to ask Hansel and Gretel why they used *bread crumbs* to mark the trail? (Come on—how well could *that* work?) Or ask Cinderella why she didn't speak up to those overbearing sisters? Here's a chance for your students to do just that by becoming part of the story.

Palatini, Margie. *Piggie Pie!* Illustrated by Howard Fine. 1995. New York: Houghton Mifflin. ISBN: 0-395-86618-9.

SATIRICAL PICTURE BOOK (PRIMARY THROUGH HIGH SCHOOL)

SUMMARY: A rollicking good story of a not-too-quick-on-her-broom witch outwitted by a bunch of very on-their-toes pigs. This book can be read on several levels. Younger reader-writers will enjoy watching how Gritch the Witch get her just deserts (and *not* desserts!). Older reader-writers will appreciate the satirical humor and the jabs at fairy tale traditions.

**Voice
65**

LESSON IDEA: The humor gives Palatini's story much of its voice, but in the end, the dialogue is the frosting on the cake. To see how much difference dialogue makes, first, read Palatini's book a second time, asking students to listen especially for dialogue (explain to younger students what dialogue is, so everyone understands what to listen for). Then, brainstorm words to describe Gritch the Witch simply based on how she talks. Now, re-tell a simple story (e.g., "The Three Bears") in a few sentences, just summarizing the plot, using no dialogue whatsoever. Put your "simple" version, in big print, plenty of space between lines, on the overhead, where students can watch you work. Ask them for suggestions on dialogue to round out the story. You will need to prompt younger writers; older writers will leap to the challenge. (Hint: Do NOT re-create the original; come up with your own fresh dialogue.) When you're finished, retype your revised dialogue version and read both so students can hear the difference. Then post them.

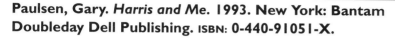

Paulsen, Gary. *Harris and Me.* 1993. New York: Bantam Doubleday Dell Publishing. ISBN: 0-440-91051-X.

FICTIONAL AUTOBIOGRAPHY (ELEMENTARY, MIDDLE SCHOOL)

SUMMARY: For read-aloud books, this one is hard to beat. You may have to put it down at moments to recover. The characters, especially Harris, Glennis, and Louie, are truly unforgettable. By the end of the book, you *know* these people. Gary's actual parents, as many fans know, were alcoholics, and Gary was often sent to live with relatives for extended periods. This is the account of one summer spent with the family of cousin Harris, daredevil and inventor of wild schemes extraordinaire. Gary is just, shall we say, along for the wild ride—and he barely survives.

LESSON IDEA: Because this is such a fine read-aloud book, that truly is enough. But you may wish to ask students, as they listen, where the voice comes from. (Giving them photocopies of a section to mark up is helpful in this process.) Paulsen is a great one for realizing that what is funniest in life is almost never totally funny. It's part nostalgia, wistfulness, sadness—or sheer terror. All play a role in this book. As you read, ask students to look carefully at their own copy, putting a little X in the righthand margin each time the voice comes through very strongly. This will help them tune into their own voice. As they share in writing groups, ask them to note for one another the moments that stand out because of voice. (What's happening in the plot when the voice is strong?)

Paulsen, Gary. *Puppies, Dogs, and Blue Northers: Reflections on Being Raised by a Pack of Sled Dogs*. 1996. New York: Harcourt Brace & Company. ISBN: 0-15-292881-2.

NONFICTION CHAPTER BOOK/JOURNAL (PRIMARY THROUGH HIGH SCHOOL)

SUMMARY: This timeless book, by turns hilarious and poignant, shows off the impressive range of Paulsen's voice. Read it first yourself, then choose passages to share aloud. It's an obvious choice for teaching voice, but would work for *any* trait. It's highly fluent, and wonderfully detailed, as engaging as any fictional piece. Though written at a level adults can enjoy, this book enthralls even the youngest readers.

LESSON IDEA: Write to Gary (you can write through the publisher; the address is available at any bookstore). Letters are an excellent way of learning and building voice, and within the letter, you can comment on *his* voice, style, humor, fluency, or any other salient features of the book. Gary has an agent who screens his mail, and he's good about responding.

Paulsen, Gary. *Soldier's Heart*. 1998. New York: Bantam Doubleday Dell Publishing Group. ISBN: 0-385-32498-7.

HISTORY-BASED CHAPTER BOOK (MIDDLE SCHOOL, HIGH SCHOOL)

SUMMARY: This book is part fiction, part historical fact. Though not every event happened just as told, the basic events of the Civil War are recounted as they occurred, and Charlie Goddard, the primary character, was a real person. He lied about his age in order to enlist in the First Minnesota Volunteers at the age of 15, fought through most of the war, and survived it. He died shortly after this experience, at the age of 23, from stress. He had what has come to be known as "soldier's heart." One of Paulsen's finest works, rich with voice and true to its subject. An excellent introduction to any study of the Civil War, and an especially good lead-in to *The Red Badge of Courage,* which it strongly resembles, though it's simpler to get hold of.

LESSON IDEA: Discussion: Note Paulsen's "Selected Sources" on pp. 105–106 of the book. How much research does it take to create a good book, even when part of it is fiction? **Alternatives:** This book is written in third person, yet we know Charlie's attitude and frame of mind change through his harrowing experiences. Invite students to create a series of letters reflecting this. Or, see if you can find someone who has experienced war to do an interview (press conference style) with your class in which they share their experiences and respond to questions. Students might follow up with an interview summary, news story, editorial, or video—with the presenter's approval, of course.

Polacco, Patricia. *Thank You, Mr. Falker.* 1998. New York: Philomel Books. ISBN: 0-399-23166-8.

PICTURE BOOK (PRIMARY THROUGH HIGH SCHOOL)

SUMMARY: This is a book sure to touch the heart of anyone who has had difficulty learning to read (or do anything for that matter), or who has tried to help someone else learn. It paints a crystal clear picture of heartless rejection and the abject despair that can come from feeling helpless and different. Polacco's story is crushing in its power—but filled with hope and joy at the end. All the more so (on both sides) because it is true.

LESSON IDEA: As you read the book aloud, ask students to keep a record of moments when the voice is strongest for them. See if they agree at the end. Is voice a steady hum—or more of a drum beat that comes and goes? Suppose this story, Polacco's own, were written up as a factual report, journalistic style? What would be lost in terms of the voice? (Try it and see!)

Robinson, Aminah Brenda Lynn. *A Street Called Home.* 1997. New York: Harcourt Brace & Company. ISBN: 0-15-201465-9.

ACCORDION-STYLE FOLD-OUT PICTURE BOOK (PRIMARY THROUGH MIDDLE SCHOOL)

SUMMARY: Unique and glorious. This enchanting book unfolds, accordian fashion, into an actual cardboard "street" with little character-faced doors that open to reveal descriptions of each character. It's a book and playhouse all in one (children of all ages, 8 to 80, love it), and an invitation to do personal interviews, a form that connects naturally to voice.

LESSON IDEA: Begin by reading the book and talking about the details that bring each character to life, unfolding the "street" as you go. Then, create a street of your own! Start with a long piece of butcher paper on which you can draw the community you wish to represent: your room, your school, your street, your town, etc. Students can do this together, using sketches, collages, photos—or a combination. Now for the really fun part: making the character windows. Younger students might create pictorial self-portraits. Paste, glue or staple them on one side, so they can open like little doors. Behind the doors, put a dictated or child-created biography. It doesn't need to be long. Ask older students to interview each other, then write slightly longer, but concise descriptions to go behind the doors. **Extension:** To build even stronger interview skills, ask students to interview other teachers or personnel in your building, or people within the community. *Stretch . . .* make your street long and rich with characters!

Rothman, Tony, Ph.D. *Instant Physics: From Aristotle to Einstein, and Beyond.* 1995. New York: Random House. ISBN: 449-90697-3.

NONFICTION CHAPTER BOOK (HIGH SCHOOL)

SUMMARY: Anyone who begins a book on physics this way—"Now, onward. Enlightenment awaits! Let's rock and roll"—has got to win your heart. I never rocked or rolled in physics, or understood much of it for that matter. I won't mislead anyone by saying this is the simplest book on earth if you do not know physics. But I can follow most of it, and I can surely appreciate the lengths Dr. Rothman goes to in making himself clear and *interesting.* He doesn't try to be Dave Barry, but he's definitely not encyclopedic, either. Don't let the formulas scare you; you can get a lot out of this book without knowing a single one. And if you're a physics student or teacher, the explanations will likely surpass anything in your textbook for clarity.

LESSON IDEA: Choose a passage you think is well done. Assess it for clarity on a 1–5 or 1–6 scale. **Alternative:** Using the same passage, create your own rubric, coming up with at least three traits you feel are important in technical writing. Define at least three levels of performance for each trait: *Strong, Developing,* and *Beginning.* You may also wish to compare Rothman's passage to a comparable passage from any physics textbook. How are they alike and different. Which is better writing? Why? What role does voice play in your choice?

San Francisco Writerscorps, editors. *Same Difference: Young Writers on Race.* **1999. San Francisco: WritersCorps Books.** ISBN: 1-888048-03-4.

POETRY BY STUDENTS (ELEMENTARY THROUGH HIGH SCHOOL)

SUMMARY: Arresting, insightful, and creative, this is a collection not to be missed. Read poems aloud and you'll be teaching both fluency and voice—ideas, too, for the thoughts are provocative, sometimes shocking, and profound. The feelings are sharp, right on the edge.

LESSON IDEA: Invite students to perform poems aloud, individually or in groups. A group might select several poems with similar themes and do them as choral readings. Of course, these poems are likely to inspire students to write poems of their own. Their honesty touches us and gives us courage to be honest, too. You may also wish to discuss the feelings unveiled here: What do your students learn? Are there surprises? Which voices speak to them?

Voice 69

Scieszka, Jon. *Math Curse.* **Illustrated by Lane Smith. 1995. New York: Viking.** ISBN: 0-670-86194-4.

PICTURE BOOK (PRIMARY THROUGH HIGH SCHOOL)

SUMMARY: Almost everyone from age 5 on up loves this zany look at the world through the eyes of a young boy coping with a "math curse." Through the course of his wild, wacky, and mathematically troublesome day, we discover that everything *is* indeed a math problem. Read it aloud just for fun or do a little more.

LESSON IDEA: Don't *most* of us feel this way—if not about math, then about *something*? Homework? Dieting? Exercise? Computers? Traffic? Shopping? Cleaning house? Taxes? Sure! So after sharing the book, use it as a spin-off for writing: Students can create their own "_____ Curse." Don't forget illustrations, which can be just as full of voice as the text. Take time to really enjoy them in Scieszka and Lane's original.

Starbright Foundation Staff, editors. *The Emperor's New Clothes: An All-Star Illustrated Retelling of the Classic Fairy Tale.* **1998. New York: Harcourt Brace and Company.** ISBN: 0-15-100436-6.

SATIRICAL RETELLING OF THE CLASSIC FAIRY TALE IN MULTIPLE VOICES (MIDDLE SCHOOL, HIGH SCHOOL)

SUMMARY: Numerous celebrities—Liam Neeson, Angela Lansbury, Dr. Ruth, Penny Marshall, Robin Williams, Jason Alexander, Steven Spielberg,

John Lithgow, and others—lent their writing talents to this retelling, and it's a treasure. Instead of being written in one voice, from one point of view, this ingenious book is retold from multiple points of view. We hear from the Imperial Prime Minister, the weavers, the court jester, the mirror, the Empress, the Emperor, the honest boy (and his mother), the spinning wheel—in short, everyone who has a role to play. Illustrations by such well-known and gifted artists as Maurice Sendak, Quentin Blake, Chris Van Allsburg and Tomie dePaola add to the fun in this witty, lively romp. It can be shared for fun on a literal level, but it's also an excellent piece for teaching satire, and well-suited to readers' theater.

LESSON IDEA: Read the book aloud if you wish, or better yet, assign parts and let your students read and enact the play, for that's what it is. If you (and they) are ambitious, you can choose a well-known tale of your own, brainstorm all the parts (think carefully; stories have more "characters" than you think!), and retell the tale, asking each student to write his/her part *only,* from a very personal point of view. Make sure everyone knows the basic plot first, so your story doesn't lose continuity. This is a complex task. Great fun, though, and a real challenge even for sophisticated high schoolers.

Steig, William. *Grown-Ups Get to Do All the Driving.* **1995. New York: HarperCollins Publishers. ISBN: 0-06-205080-X.**

CARTOON COLLECTION (PRIMARY THROUGH HIGH SCHOOL)

SUMMARY: It is one thing to be the parent of a child, and quite another to *be* the child, and to see the world as he or she does. So, what do children think of us grown-ups? Steig shows us some insights, and some gently humorous differences of opinion in how the real world runs. He also invites us to step back and look at ourselves, and laugh (we *are* ridiculous, you know).

LESSON IDEA: Once students have had an opportunity to look at the book and appreciate kids' comments on just how grownups live and think, they may wish to create their own version. This is an ideal class project, with each student doing one cartoon with a caption—all from the same perspective: teachers get to do all the testing, older kids get out of all the chores, parents get to pick all the TV shows, babies get all the attention, etc. When you finish and share or display results, talk about the impact of perspective on voice.

Steptoe, John. *Creativity.* **Illustrated by E.B. Lewis. 1997.**
New York: Houghton Mifflin Company. ISBN: 0-395-68706-3.

PICTURE BOOK (ELEMENTARY, MIDDLE SCHOOL)

SUMMARY: Like Daniel Pinkwater's *The Big Orange Splot,* this book deals with individuality, but this time in a more serious way. Charles and Hector, the two primary characters, have much in common, yet they're different, or so they think at first. After all, Charles is black, and much of his language is street talk, while Hector, the new kid, is from Puerto Rico, is only partly black, and has straight hair. He also has a tendency to wear the "wrong" clothes and shoes, something Charles sets out to correct. Along the way, they both discover the true meaning of creativity: being yourself, in your speech, your hairstyle, your body language, your clothing, or whatever. Just you. The real thing.

LESSON IDEA: Ask students to think of people they know, living or dead, who might be considered "creative" in the sense intended by John Steptoe's book. They might be historical figures, personalities, writers, sports stars, presidents, or people known personally to a particular student. Ask students to use lists or word webs to generate reasons that each person might be considered "creative," or individual. Give students time for some personal research on the individuals they have chosen. Then, ask them to write a short description, a paragraph or two, explaining that person's "creativity." Share the writings aloud to talk about ways other creative people have expressed who they are. **Alternative:** You can also celebrate individual creativity by having a day in which each person brings to class a special possession, piece of music or art, poem, piece of clothing or any item he/she feels best expresses his/her own creativity.

Voice
71

Wisniewski, David. *Tough Cookie.* **1999. New York: Lothrop,**
Lee & Shepard Books. ISBN: 0-688-15337-2.

PICTURE BOOK (ELEMENTARY THROUGH HIGH SCHOOL)

SUMMARY: How many crime stories take place inside a cookie jar? Right. When David Wisniewski says his hero's a tough cookie, he isn't messing around. It's the truth. This book has some fun with the detective genre of the 1930s and 1940s, a la Humphrey Bogart. Students who have studied film from this era—or at least seen a detective film from this time—will especially appreciate this very light-hearted send-off. But the story is funny even without the depth this background provides. The villain is (you guessed it) Fingers. Hmm.

Can Tough Cookie ward him off with only Pecan Sandy and a handful of crumbs on his side? Fingers is ruthless. Tough times are ahead.

LESSON IDEA: This book takes its voice from 1940s gangster movies. But there are many other possibilities your students may have fun exploring: e.g., the "Clueless" valley girl voice, or the voice of Austin Powers. Ask them to choose a voice and to write a brief story using that voice. If this is difficult, take a story you already know—"Little Red Riding Hood"—and re-tell it using a new voice. (See also Shaquille O'Neal, *Shaq and the Beanstalk,* from this section, for additional ideas.)

Yolen, Jane. *Sleeping Ugly.* **Illustrated by Diane Stanley. 1981. New York: Penguin Putnam. ISBN: 0-698-11560-0.**

VIC'S PICKS

PICTURE BOOK (PRIMARY THROUGH HIGH SCHOOL)

Voice 72

SUMMARY: Younger students will love this hilarious tale of poor, loveable Plain Jane, the wretched Princess Miserella, and the greatest magic-making fairy this side of an enchanted forest. Older students will appreciate the satirical, playful approach to the fairy tale genre, and may be inspired to imitate it. Clever enough to amuse even adult audiences.

LESSON IDEA: Just reading this book aloud is enough; it simply rings with voice, and is a delight to share. But if you wish to take it a step further, you might invite older reader/writers to act out one of the scenes; the confrontation with Miserella in Plain Jane's cabin comes to mind. Some writers may also feel challenged to try a new version of an old fairy tale—anything out of Grimm or Andersen will do—taking some liberties, of course, with tradition.

Books for Teaching

Word Choice

Careful writers choose just the right word or phrase to make meaning clear or to create a particular mood or feeling within a piece of writing. That is the essence of good word choice. The books in this section are designed both to help expand students' vocabulary, and to illustrate the power of language that is used with precision. Many of the books in this section were chosen because they use simple language with striking clarity. Others stretch the reader's knowledge of language with unusual expressions or specialized language from a particular content area, such as biology. Each provides read-aloud opportunities to serve as models for students' own writing.

Teach word choice by

- Reading aloud
- Collecting favorite words/phrases
- Building word collages
- "Burying" tired, worn out phrases
- Finding "10 other ways to say it"
- Choosing words to suit audience and purpose

Angier, Natalie. *The Beauty of the Beastly: New Views on the Nature of Life.* 1995. New York: Houghton Mifflin. ISBN: **0-395-79147-2.**

NONFICTION CHAPTER BOOK ON SCIENCE (MIDDLE SCHOOL, HIGH SCHOOL)

SUMMARY: Angier finds beauty in the creatures most of us find repulsive, and also finds eloquent and vivid ways to describe them: her hyenas, for instance, have an "espresso brown face" that is "both tender and strong." (p. 138) The language in this book is exceptional, and Angier also manages to weave a bit of humor into her informational writing. She is a Pulitzer Prize winner and Lewis Thomas Book Award winner. You'll see why.

LESSON IDEA: After listening to sections from the book, ask students to select a creature they find truly repulsive. Then, for a week or so, they should dig up all the information they can on this creature. Keep voluminous notes; then choose the 10 most interesting findings. Turn them into an informational essay or brochure, poem, or introductory informational piece for a zoo or other natural exhibit at which this creature might appear. Think about audience, and write a piece that is appropriately formal or informal, technical or nontechnical. **Option:** Write a piece from the *creature's point of view.* **Extension:** After sharing writings, talk about any changes in attitude produced by the research and/or the writing.

Edwards, Pamela Duncan. *Some Smug Slug.* Illustrated by Henry Cole. 1996. New York: HarperCollins Publishers. ISBN: **0-06-024789-4.**

PICTURE BOOK (PRIMARY THROUGH HIGH SCHOOL)

SUMMARY: "One summer Sunday, while strolling on soil, with its antennae signaling, a slug sensed a slope." All S's, sure, but sense is certainly never sacrificed to sound! Not for a second! Indeed, the vocabulary is wondrously varied; expect student listeners of any age to master a whole host of new words and expressions, all the while savoring this saucy tale of strategy and surprise.

LESSON IDEA: This book is a good starting point for creating your own text—story, poem, advertisement, poster, whatever—featuring the letter-sound combination of your choice. This is NOT just for young students, by the way; this activity will challenge even the most experienced student writers.

Florian, Douglas. *Insectlopedia.* 1998. New York: Harcourt Brace & Company. ISBN: 0-15-201306-7.

POETIC PICTURE BOOK WITH WATERCOLOR ART
(PRIMARY THROUGH HIGH SCHOOL)

SUMMARY: This could be a coffee table book; it's that beautiful. But you'll want to read the poems too, aloud, of course, and more than once. Talk about whimsical use of language (as in the opening to the Caterpillar poem): "She eats eight leaves at least/To fill her,/Which **leaves** her like a/Fatterpillar . . ." See how the very first poem hooks you.

LESSON IDEA: The language in this book must be shared. Invite students to participate in reader's theater, or to do a choral reading of the entire book (wonderful imagery and strong verbs invite dramatic interpretation). While you're at it, notice layout, too: the arching inchworm or the circling whirligig beetles. The balance of text and picture is inviting to both eye and ear.

See also

- Florian, Douglas. *Beast Feast.* 1994. New York: Harcourt Brace. ISBN: 0-15-295178-4. Equally wonderful.

Fox, Mem. *Feathers and Fools.* Illustrated by Nicholas Wilton. 1996. New York: Harcourt Brace. ISBN: 0-15-200473-4.

PICTURE BOOK (PRIMARY THROUGH HIGH SCHOOL)

SUMMARY: This is one of Mem Fox's most beautiful books. It has an elegant vocabulary that invites—almost demands—multiple readings, especially for young listeners. One way to assess their understanding is to ask them to re-write or re-tell the story in simpler words. The plot is a simple and timeless one: war between groups who do not understand one another. The language, on the other hand, invites thought and inference.

LESSON IDEA: Linger over some favorite words, perhaps jotting them down or making a collection. Brainstorm synonyms or related words for favorites. Talk about some of Mem's choices: What do we picture when she says the peacocks "pecked and strutted"? What are "anxious mutterings"? What's a "way of life"? What are "fighting words"? What sort of feeling is "dismay"? When do you feel it? What does she mean when she says "a cloud of feathers . . . haunted the sun"? It's easy to read this book too fast and to skip over these rich phrases. Ask students, in pairs or groups, to contemplate Mem's delicious word choice, and to infer possible meanings from context. Also ask them to explain how they came up with those meanings (the "how" is often the most interesting part of the answer). If answers are not all the same, so much the better! Then you can talk about multiple meanings. **Alternative:** Put students into "interpretive groups" of two or three, and have each group responsible for interpreting and explaining the significance of *one page* of this complex text.

Word Choice
76

Gordon, David George. *The Compleat Cockroach*. 1996. Berkeley, CA: Ten Speed Press. ISBN: 0-89815-853-2.

NONFICTION CHAPTER BOOK ON SCIENCE (MIDDLE SCHOOL, HIGH SCHOOL)

SUMMARY: Did you know that cockroaches taste like shrimp (p. 47), that they have been ingredients in medicine (p. 51), that Americans alone spend $500 million per year trying to kill them (p. 164), or that they can sing (p. 68)? Well, you can learn all this—and much more—from Gordon's readable, well-researched book. It's a model of clarity, with language that is technically correct where necessary, but never jargonistic or inflated. The sentences are clear, crisp, and easy to follow. Also consider it as a model of fine layout. As you leaf through, notice the use of photographs, shaded sketches, sidebars and subheads.

LESSON IDEA: Why not combine good word choice with a lesson in presentation and layout? Ask students to research and write the informational copy first, on any topic of their choice. Criteria: The copy *must* include a minimum of five pieces of information *not likely to have been previously known* to other members of the class. Next, ask them to present it effectively, using a visually appealing style: poster, illustrated report, brochure, letter—or? They may use illustrations, sketches, sidebars, graphs, etc., to enhance the presentation. Criterion for assessment: Does the presentation *make those five key points stand out*?

Kacirk, Jeffrey. *Forgotten English*. 1997. New York: William Morrow and Company. ISBN: 0-688-16636-9.

ANNOTATED DICTIONARY OF OUT-OF-DATE WORDS (MIDDLE SCHOOL, HIGH SCHOOL)

SUMMARY: A great browsing book. Called a "merry guide to antiquated words," and so it is. It's also a lesson on how English is changing and why.

Some words never really catch on. Perhaps they're too long, too hard to remember, or too difficult to spell! Seen a *terebinth* lately? Had a sip of *sillyebubbe*? Spoken with the *bee-master*? If you aren't sure, you need this book.

LESSON IDEA: Kacirk definitely invites some creative game playing to see who can guess the correct meaning of these antiquated words. You can use the words to play "fictionary," a game in which students who know the definition of a word invent two false definitions to see if they can stump two or three other students within a small group. You get a point each time you guess right, and another point for each teammate you stump. **Extension:** Ask students to do a little dictionary exploration on their own. No need to stick to Webster; bring in some specialized dictionaries with technical terminology, medical terminology, etc. Ask each student to choose one word he/she thinks will fall into oblivion in the next 100 years, and one that will still be with us. And to explain why. Want more of a challenge? Ask each student to invent a word we really need in English, one that could take on a life of its own: e.g., What could we call those potholes they keep repairing that come back and back . . . ? Create a class dictionary of your new, useful words.

Lederer, Richard. *Crazy English: The Ultimate Joy Ride Through Our Language*. 1998. New York: Simon and Schuster. ISBN: 0-671-02323-3.

Chapter Book on the English Language (Middle School, High School)

SUMMARY: If the plural of *mouse* is *mice,* then why aren't *houses hice*? English is a wild and unpredictable language, probably much more so than you realize until you explore this very funny but informative book. You'll see the longest word in our language (1,913 letters—put that one on the old weekly spelling quiz). You'll learn about some zany grammatical structures, too, along with oddities in spelling, phobias of virtually every type, strange figurative language, and a host of other things from the beautiful to the funky.

LESSON IDEA: This is a browsing book, not a read-through book, by its nature. You *will* want to share some sections aloud, but it is also important to *see* certain parts—on spelling, for instance—to appreciate them. If you can have more than one copy in your classroom, your students will enjoy it. It's not a workbook or textbook—more of a collection of word jokes. It's an excellent book for kicking off group projects on the quirky nature of English, which might focus on one of these topics: unexpected spellings, trademark names often used (incorrectly and illegally!) as common nouns, borrowed words (we're the heaviest borrowers on earth—one reason our language is so big), phobias, and words with meanings you wouldn't predict.

Lovett, Sarah. *Extremely Weird Sea Creatures*. Illustrated by Mary Sundstrom and Beth Evans. 1992. Santa Fe, NM: John Muir Publications. ISBN: 1-56261-287-5.

NONFICTION PICTURE BOOK (ELEMENTARY, MIDDLE SCHOOL)

SUMMARY: Much of the language in this remarkably well-done book is highly sophisticated. But aren't reading specialists telling us to help young readers stretch by going over their heads a bit? Lovett uses language so well, and her text is so well-illustrated, that you should not hesitate to use it with young readers, who will find her choice of creatures captivating. Here's a sample: "If you had feet growing out of your head, you might be known as a head-footed animal. Of course, it would take more than that to qualify you as a member of the class Cephalopoda, or 'head-foots.'" Now you're beginning to know what "cephalopoda" means (if you didn't previously), and Lovett made it pretty easy, too. This technical book reflects lots of audience sensitivity; Lovett writes just as you hope your students will.

LESSON IDEA: Pick a word or two from a given article you plan to read aloud. *Cephalopod* would be a good choice for our sample chapter. Give students some time to play with possible definitions of this word, in groups. Ask them to write out hypothetical definitions. Then, listen to the article, and re-think those definitions, first through discussion, then through writing. Also talk about how the writer makes ideas clear: e.g., examples, analogies, synonyms, using words in context, illustrations.

Marshall, James. *Swine Lake*. Illustrated by Maurice Sendak. 1999. New York: HarperCollins Publishers. ISBN: 0-06-205171-7.

VIC'S PICKS

SATIRICAL PICTURE BOOK (PRIMARY THROUGH HIGH SCHOOL)

SUMMARY: A hilarious send-off of "Swan Lake," but also a tribute to the magical effect of theater, even on one so jaded as Mr. Wolf, who attends only to seize a quick dinner (one of the actors, no less), and finds himself quite— well—swept away by the on-stage action.

LESSON IDEA: When you read the book aloud, ask students to list favorite words or phrases, including those that might be new to them. Younger students may wish to guess at the meaning from context; and you may wish to create a glossary for this word-rich text. **Alternatives:** Older students may have fun doing a reader's theater version of this tongue-in-cheek piece. Notice it ends with a review of the wolf's performance; don't omit this important piece from your oral reading! As an extension, you may wish to have your students write additional reviews (great practice in persuasive writing), or even do an oral review with a "Siskel & Ebert" format, offering different opinions on the wolf's finer moments on stage.

Paulsen, Gary. *Canoe Days*. Illustrated by Ruth Wright Paulsen. 1999. New York: Bantam Doubleday Dell. ISBN: 0-385-32524-X.

PICTURE BOOK (PRIMARY THROUGH MIDDLE SCHOOL)

SUMMARY: A beautiful book with a strong reverence for nature, this text also gives us a lesson on the value of simple language used eloquently: "The water is a window into the skylake." Paulsen always makes it look so easy.

LESSON IDEA: Paulsen writes about a "canoe day" because canoeing is one of his favorite activities. After reading the book, ask students to recall as many details as they can that made this canoe day so special. Then, ask them to think of a kind of day—snow day, dog day, hiking day—that would be special to *them* for whatever reason. Now, ask each person to list as many words, phrases or images as he/she can connected to that special day. Then, ask them to write a short text, illustrated if they like, about the special day. For younger students, pick one kind of day to do as a group; brainstorm together, and create pictures or picture-text combinations. Assemble the results in a book or display them.

Pinkney, Andrea Davis. *Duke Ellington*. Illustrated by Brian Pinkney. 1998. New York: Hyperion Books for Children. ISBN: 0-7868-0178-6.

BIOGRAPHICAL PICTURE BOOK (ELEMENTARY, MIDDLE SCHOOL)

SUMMARY: "Yeah, those solos were kickin'. Hot-buttered bop, with lots of sassy-cool tunes." The originality and richness of the language in this poetic biography is as irresistible as the music of the man it celebrates. And it fits so beautifully. Toby the sax player is "curling his notes like a kite tail in the wind." This isn't difficult language; it's just used with spice and love, the love of words that make meaning in the way the right notes make music so sweet you just have to hear it again.

LESSON IDEA: Read the piece aloud and ask students to pick out some of their favorite phrases. It won't be hard! List them on the overhead. Talk about why simple language often works well when it's used in a new way—*hot-buttered* and *sassy cool*. **Extension:** If you wish to do more, think poetry. Begin with an image: a tree, an old hat, a worn staircase, a horse running, a dog sleeping on the porch, or whatever. Ask students to try to see the image in a new way. Perhaps the sleepy old dog on the porch becomes a giant paper-weight, holding the old house down against the force of the wind. Or the hat hugs its owner's head, fearful of being left behind, fearful of falling to the ground. Your students may not be as poetic as Pinkney (few of us are), but the point is to play with language and overstep the clichés. It takes thought.

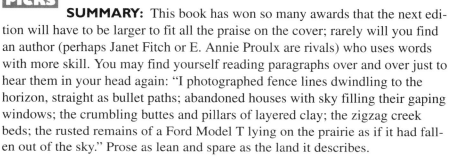

Raban, Jonathan. *Bad Land: An American Romance*. 1996. New York: Random House. ISBN: 0-679-75906-9.

HISTORICAL NONFICTION CHAPTER BOOK (HIGH SCHOOL)

SUMMARY: This book has won so many awards that the next edition will have to be larger to fit all the praise on the cover; rarely will you find an author (perhaps Janet Fitch or E. Annie Proulx are rivals) who uses words with more skill. You may find yourself reading paragraphs over and over just to hear them in your head again: "I photographed fence lines dwindling to the horizon, straight as bullet paths; abandoned houses with sky filling their gaping windows; the crumbling buttes and pillars of layered clay; the zigzag creek beds; the rusted remains of a Ford Model T lying on the prairie as if it had fallen out of the sky." Prose as lean and spare as the land it describes.

LESSON IDEA: In Raban's book, the "bad land" was settled by people full of hope, recruited from another place (often the Eastern U.S.) to begin life anew on land they had no idea would be so harsh and unyielding. You might use his text as a basis to study character and its relation to time and place. Begin with photographs of people from another generation (students can pull these from family albums or from magazines). Put them on display. Study the faces. Who are they? What do you learn? Ask each student to pick one—his/her own or another—and to write in that person's voice. What is the person in the picture thinking or feeling? **Alternative:** Ask students to write a brochure that invites people to leave their homes for a "new land of promise." What kind of language do you need to use to persuade people to make such a life-altering decision? Compare the language and voice from these two kinds of writing: How are they different?

Rice, Scott, editor. *It Was a Dark and Stormy Night: the Final Conflict*. 1992. New York: Penguin Books. ISBN: 0-14-015791-3.

COLLECTION OF ENTRIES FROM THE BULWER-LYTTON FICTION CONTEST (MIDDLE SCHOOL, HIGH SCHOOL)

SUMMARY: If you have students who sometimes overwrite (jargon, modifier-fest, romance novel syndrome, etc.), this is your book. Inventive and hilarious.

Select a few choice over-done-it's to illustrate when enough is enough. You *will* need to screen; there's some ribald fun in this one.

LESSON IDEA: Read aloud—and even invite students to mark up the text. Talk about the whole concept of "overwriting." Why do people do it? Why doesn't it work—usually? **Extensions:** Rewrite a few of the *worst* examples to see what happens when you tone down the language. Have students look for samples of overwriting; make a collection of your own to display. Best of all, have your own Bulwer-Lytton contest to see who can do the most overwritten lead to "Moby Dick," or "The Tell-Tale Heart" or the most overwritten description of a sunset or beauty product (ads are good examples; many are right on the edge as it is). You could also work on the most overdone resume, recipe, dialogue for a sit-com, or introduction to any textbook. Have fun: the serene sky's the absolute overriding limit as we fade blissfully into the shimmering shadows that threaten to overtake the fair and sunny meanderings of our golden far-ranging thoughts . . .

Snicket, Lemony. *A Series of Unfortunate Events: The Bad Beginning (Book I)*. 1999. New York: HarperCollins Publishers. ISBN: 0-06-440766-7.

CHAPTER BOOK (MIDDLE SCHOOL)

SUMMARY: The voice in this book is difficult to characterize; perhaps it's a combination of Dickens and Roald Dahl, with a touch of E. B. White for flavor. It's a good bet that a writer with a name like Lemony Snicket will not be boring—and he's not. You can tell what you're in for from the book jacket alone: "It is my sad duty to write down these unpleasant tales, but there is nothing stopping you from putting this book down at once and reading something happy, if you prefer that sort of thing." Well, who in his/her right mind would prefer that? And Snicket delivers, with constant surprises—many unpleasant, yes, but none so challenging that his stalwart, endlessly resourceful heroes (all children) cannot handle them. Warning: This book is addictive (part of a series, thankfully).

LESSON IDEA: As you read the book aloud, you'll notice the ingenious and deft way in which Snicket handles vocabulary—he's never overbearing about it, but he manages to weave in a brief lesson or two as he goes along, and they're entertaining, even if you know the words. Writing in context is an effective way to teach vocabulary—if students do not have to handle too many words at once. Give them a word list of up to 20 words, but ask them to choose only two or three from the list. Then ask them to write a brief passage imitating Snicket's well-crafted strategy of not only using words well, but defining for us just *how* he is using each one in a particular passage. Words have nuances of meaning, and Snicket makes this abundantly clear. Can your students do the same? Note: Excellent books for reluctant readers. They are short and filled with suspense, excellent dialogue, humor, and wily twists of fate.

Stegner, Wallace. *Where the Bluebird Sings to the Lemonade Springs.* 1993. New York: Penguin Books. ISBN: 0-14-017402-8.

ESSAY COLLECTION (HIGH SCHOOL)

SUMMARY: To pick up this book is to lose yourself in a sea of hauntingly beautiful prose: 16 essays by Wallace Stegner on life in the West. The book is a combination of memoir, keen observation, philosophy, and expository writing based on a lifetime of personal research. Rich with imagery, it's a gem to use in teaching detail, but also ideal for word choice because Stegner's vocabulary is astounding and challenging, even to the well-read. He moves with razor-sharp precision through his landscape portraits—Gene Kelly dancing across the plateaus of our Western imagination.

LESSON IDEA: Choose several sections to read aloud just for the pleasure of it. Pass out copies students can see and mark up. Then, ask them to work in pairs or small groups to identify favorite phrases, or those that puzzle them. Work on the puzzling ones, coming up with the best definitions from context that you can. **Extension:** Ask students to select one favorite word or phrase to use in the opening of a piece of their own, using any associations Stegner's text calls to mind.

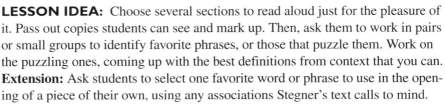

Steig, Jeanne. *Consider the Lemming.* Illustrated by William Steig. 1988. New York: Farrar, Straus and Giroux. ISBN: 0-374-41361-4.

POETRY COLLECTION (ELEMENTARY THROUGH HIGH SCHOOL)

SUMMARY: Jeanne Steig writes of the camel: "Although his back's commodious/His disposition's idious." When words are used with such flair and inventiveness, you love reading the text aloud and pausing to reflect on the perfect word choice. Perhaps that's what those funny little people on the cover are doing.

LESSON IDEA: Do your students know the word *transmogrification*? When they read Steig's poem "The Weasel," chances are good they'll figure it out. Ask students to jot down and save favorite words or phrases while listening to these very witty poems. In some cases, you may wish to talk about word meanings, seeing first if students can guess from context. The vocabulary is sophisticated, despite the very light tone. Create a class glossary and post it, inviting students to use Steig's words, too. You may also wish to talk about her unlikely rhymes: *has* and *razzmatazz.* This isn't hum-drum vocab. **Extension:** Want a challenge? Ask students to identify two words that rhyme, whether they relate in any way or not. Then, pass the two rhyming words to a partner, who will see if she/he can incorporate them into a poem! Have fun, but don't take it too seriously; Jeanne Steig is a very tough act to follow. (Note: The topic does not need to be animals.)

Stewart, Ian. *Nature's Numbers.* 1995. New York: HarperCollins Publishers. ISBN: 0-465-07273-9.

NONFICTION CHAPTER BOOK ON MATH (HIGH SCHOOL)

SUMMARY: "I am going to take you sightseeing in that mathematical universe. I am going to try to equip you with a mathematician's eyes. And by so doing, I shall do my best to change the way you view your own world." So begins Stewart's wonderful venture into the world of thinking mathematically—seeing patterns in the universe and using them to solve puzzles. You don't have to be a mathematician to love this book. You just have to be a person who loves clear thinking, well expressed.

LESSON IDEA: Not all math texts are equally well-written. Assemble a variety, extract some explanations, and compare them with each other and with excerpts from Stewart. Assess them for ideas (clarity), sentence structure, and word choice/terminology, using the *informational* rubric. Discuss the why's of your results. **Extension:** Draft a job announcement for a math textbook writer.

Van Allsburg, Chris. *The Z Was Zapped.* 1987. New York: Houghton Mifflin. ISBN: 0-395-44612-0.

ALPHABET BOOK (PRIMARY THROUGH MIDDLE SCHOOL)

SUMMARY: In this highly creative alphabet book, letters encounter various mishaps, but we're left to guess what the exact problem is until we turn the page. The mishap, of course, always begins with the letter in question, narrowing our guesswork. And Van Allsburg's creative illustrations provide more clues. A joy to read and share because it is highly interactive.

LESSON IDEA: Read the book aloud, sharing pictures and encouraging plenty of guessing before you reveal each answer (some do suggest several possibilities—*students can be right without agreeing with the original*). Van Allsburg calls this book a play in 26 acts. Why not let older students portray it that way, coming up with their own words, of course. Perhaps the A could be "anchored," the D could be "demolished," and so on. As each "letter" portrays its fate, other members of the class can see if they can guess the right word. Younger students may have fun simply creating an imitative picture book version of their own (one or two letters to a student). **Extension:** For more of a challenge, connect the alphabet to a content area—math, science, whatever. The B was "bisected," the C was "calculated," the D was "divided," and so on. Each student can do one or two letters, not the whole alphabet!

van Kampen, Vlasta. *Beetle Bedlam.* 1997. Watertown, MA: Charlesbridge Publishing. ISBN: 0-88106-695-8.

FACT-BASED PICTURE BOOK (ELEMENTARY THROUGH HIGH SCHOOL)

SUMMARY: Few books are more imaginative than this one. The bark beetle is put on trial for killing trees. Various other beetles—including the harlequin beetle, the hungry tiger beetle, and the Hercules beetle—are called to testify. As they give their testimony, young readers learn a bit about trial procedure and much about the habits of beetles. This is excellent research transformed into story format, and the illustrations rival anything ever done by Disney studios. Don't overlook organization, either; the trial format provides a built-in organizer for moving the story forward.

LESSON IDEA: Think "verbs" as you read this book. Remember the old "said is dead" game? Ask students by either looking or listening (if you just want to share the book aloud) to see how many excellent *said*-substitutes they can see/hear as you go along. Examples: *muttered, grumbled, shouted, bellowed, demanded, sighed, whispered, growled, purred, snarled.* **Extension:** Talk about the expanded meaning such verbs add. Then, have students write a short dialogue between two characters in which the "said's" are replaced with more picturesque (and meaningful) verbs.

Wilson, Edward O. *In Search of Nature.* 1996. Washington, DC: Island Press. ISBN: 1-55963-215-1.

NONFICTION CHAPTER BOOK ON SCIENCE (MIDDLE SCHOOL, HIGH SCHOOL)

SUMMARY: This book is an excellent example of how to turn a technical topic into text accessible to a general audience. "The front of the [great white shark's] head, the snout, is tapered into a cone, a conspicuous feature giving rise to the alternative Australian name of white pointer . . . The mouth of the shark is usually set in a little clown's grin, agape and with teeth on display, bringing in a flow of water back across the gills in the fashion of a ramjet." Makes you think of clowns in a whole new way, does it not?

LESSON IDEA: Wilson makes it look simple, but he is a craftsman, as in this line: "Marriage ceremonies and temple architecture, for example, are the outcomes of numerous interlocking behaviors that result from cognitive activity with multiple culturgens." *There's* a good minilesson for you: See who can come up with the clearest translation of that statement. (Hint: Wilson views culture as a biological product.) Here's a philosophical question for your students: Some writers make everything crystal clear; others make us work for meaning. Which do you think is preferable? Why? (Good topic for a personal persuasive essay—examples are *a must!*)

Books
for Teaching
Sentence Fluency

Sentence fluency is much more than grammatical correctness. It is the
rhythm and flow of carefully structured language that makes it both easy
and pleasurable to read aloud. Poetry is particularly fluent, of course, and so
many poetry selections are included here. But well-written prose can also
have a poetic flow, whether in fiction or nonfiction; and so, a number of
prose selections have been included as well. These books are chosen for
their read-aloud value; and many are recommended for choral reading or
other similar activities in which students become the readers, practicing oral
interpretation of text. You will find that each book in this section invites
expressive interpretive reading, much the way a good film script might.

Teach sentence fluency by

- Reading aloud or asking students to read aloud
- Doing choral readings
- Listening to poetry and music
- Writing poetry and business letters
- Contrasting literary and business forms of writing
- Editing for conciseness

Sentence
Fluency
85

Allard, Harry. ¡La Señorita Nelson Ha Desaparecido! Illustrated by James Marshall. 1998. New York: Houghton Mifflin Company. ISBN: 0-395-90008-5.

SPANISH PICTURE BOOK (PRIMARY THROUGH HIGH SCHOOL)

SUMMARY: In this translation of the riotous *Miss Nelson Is Missing!,* the sweet and lovable Miss Nelson is again replaced by the menacing, hideously ugly señorita Pantano (aka, "the Swamp"). Children of all ages, 4 to 84, laugh aloud at the pictures and the antics of the world's most terrifying substitute—and the mischievous children she whips into line with just a look.

LESSON IDEA: This book is an excellent read-aloud example of vivid detail, fluency and oh, yes—voice! Native English speakers studying Spanish can have a field day translating sections of the book, and presenting them. The pictures offer great clues, and you might begin with a short vocabulary list of key words that offer additional help. No Spanish textbook around can compete with the fun of translating Allard and Marshall into English. (Don't forget to translate the "about the authors" sections, and the New York Times book review, too. **Extension:** To challenge more capable second language speakers (in English or Spanish), ask them, in teams, to create short picture books of their own, perhaps centering on *one* small school incident: a visit from a recent sub, perhaps, told from the students' point of view, *or* the sub's.

Angelou, Maya. *Phenomenal Woman: Four Poems Celebrating Women.* 1995. New York: Random House. ISBN: 0-679-43924-2.

POETRY (HIGH SCHOOL)

SUMMARY: You won't have to read far to find yourself saying, "Angelou is truly a poet to the bone." Every stanza rings with such fluency that you will find it difficult *not* to read aloud, even if you are by yourself. These words beg to be spoken, and demand every bit of inflection you can muster. That's fluency.

LESSON IDEA: Choose selected passages for read-around or choral reading presentations, and invite your students to perform them. If you read "Phenomenal Woman," talk about the attitude projected in this poem and how it affects voice. Does the fluency affect voice, too? How? An ideal book for stimulating discussion on how fluency, word choice, and voice all connect.

Extension: Try reading one of Angelou's stanzas with a flat, no-inflection voice. Can you do it? Why not? How does she pull the voice out of *you*?

Bedard, Michael. *Emily*. Illustrated by Barbara Cooney. 1992. New York: Bantam Doubleday Dell. ISBN: 0-385-30697-0.

PICTURE BOOK (ELEMENTARY, MIDDLE SCHOOL)

SUMMARY: The story is as lovely as the pictures and one that will leave you feeling you've truly peeked into the hidden world of Emily Dickinson, the poet known as "the Myth." In this story of a slowly blooming friendship between the poet and the child of a musician who is her neighbor, poetry and music blend together, like the melting snow of spring. As the young girl's father tells her, poetry is magic. You cannot really explain it.

LESSON IDEA: Use the premise of the book to explore the link between music and poetry. Play various kinds of music and ask students to expand their definitions of fluency based on what they hear. Letters are a good way of building fluency, too. Re-read Emily Dickinson's original letter to her young friend. Ask students to imagine they are that friend writing back. What would they say? Want another possibility? Ask students to read Emily's poem at the end aloud. They may also wish to imitate her style, writing a short (4 to 10 lines) poem of their own. One more idea: Emily makes the startling comment that it is her young friend who is truly poetry—not the words written on a piece of paper. What do you think she means by this? How can a person be a poem? Do people have built-in "fluency"? How can this be? Invite students, in answering these questions, to create a fluency collage, merging people, poetry, song lyrics, and anything else they think of as "fluent." Think expansively.

Sentence
Fluency
87

Berry, S. L. *E. E. Cummings*. 1993. Mankato, MN: Creative Education. ISBN: 0-88682-611-X.

POETIC BIOGRAPHY (ELEMENTARY THROUGH HIGH SCHOOL)

SUMMARY: Blending art, photographs, and poetry, this eye-catching book explores the life and times of one of our most celebrated and unusual poets: e. e. cummings. You could read the book just as a biography or just as a collection of poetry. Or, you could simply examine the art and find yourself mesmerized. Put them all together and you have a powerful examination of a person's life. This is about as multi-media as you can get and still remain between the covers of a book. Bravo.

LESSON IDEA: Think about a similar format for authors' biographies of your own. Side by side, through the text, juxtapose biographical paragraphs with snippets from the author's work. Include artwork or photographs that seem relevant, too. Perhaps quotations from contemporaries, either pertaining to the author's work, or simply to the time in which he/she lived.

See also, by the same publisher:

Emily Dickinson *Sylvia Plath*
Robert Frost *Edwin Arlington Robinson*
Langston Hughes *Walt Whitman*
Marianne Moore

Buchanan, Ken. *This House Is Made of Mud/Esta casa está heche de lodo*. Illustrated by Libba Tracy. 1991. Flagstaff, AZ: Northland Publishing. ISBN: 0-87358-580-1.

BILINGUAL PICTURE BOOK (PRIMARY THROUGH HIGH SCHOOL)

SUMMARY: A beautifully fluent book, poetic in flavor, with simple yet insightful observations about home and nature. Excellent for use in bilingual Spanish-English classrooms.

Sentence Fluency 88

LESSON IDEA: Read the book aloud in Spanish, English or both, just enjoying the flow, the beauty of the rhythms. If you want more of a challenge, invite students to translate sections of the text from English to Spanish or vice versa. Or, invite native speakers of Spanish and English to work together to create their own bilingual book, using *This House Is Made of Mud* as a model—but also keeping in mind that their book can be shorter and they can come up with their own topics!

Cisneros, Sandra. *The House on Mango Street*. 1989. New York: Random House. ISBN: 0-679-73477-5.

CHAPTER BOOK (ELEMENTARY THROUGH HIGH SCHOOL)

SUMMARY: This book is written "a las mujeres"—to the women. It is, though, for everyone. A coming of age book, written about growing up in the Hispanic quarter of Chicago. A book of life, love, disappointment, rage, grief, despair, and joy, the things we all feel yet cannot express quIte so fluently as Cisneros, whose voice is sheer music. The chapters are short and need not be read in order. Choose any one of them to illustrate the beauty of fluent writing. Read aloud often from this remarkable poetry-as-prose book.

LESSON IDEA: Try a read-around. Copy a short passage. Give it to students in groups of three to four and ask them to read it aloud, taking turns—only *don't* guide the flow. Let *them* decide when one reader will end and the next will begin. Let them continue reading till they have been through the passage multiple times, in multiple voices. Did they hear the fluency and voice coming out? Did the voice become stronger with each reading? Did the rhythms of the fluency change? How?

Carroll, Rebecca. *I Know What the Red Clay Looks Like: The Voice and Vision of Black Women Writers*. 1994. New York: Random House. ISBN: 0-517-59638-5.

BIOGRAPHICAL SKETCHES AND EXCERPTS (HIGH SCHOOL)

SUMMARY: A beautifully conceived book that skillfully combines biographical sketches of well-known African American women writers—their philosophies, their stories of success—with excerpts from some of their own favorite writings. The result is like a "very best of" collection of recordings, only you have to read them to hear the music. It's hard to decide whether the bios or the excerpts are more enticing, but together they make a flavorful package.

LESSON IDEA: With 15 writers to choose from, you can pair up to 30 students to do oral presentations on these fascinating writers. One student can focus on the biography (reading short quotations or doing a summary), one on the writer's work (again reading aloud or perhaps offering a critique or both). Students should begin with Carroll's book, but not feel bound by it. They should feel free to do their own biographical research and expand what Carroll has written—and also to read aloud from *any* of the authors' other works. Keep presentations short—about ten minutes per pair—and you'll give your class an opportunity to hear a veritable symphony of voices, one more fluent than the other, and each stylistically unique.

Sentence
Fluency
89

Clinton, Catherine, editor. *I, Too, Sing America: Three Centuries of African American Poetry*. 1998. New York: Houghton Mifflin. ISBN: 0-395-89599-5.

ILLUSTRATED COLLECTION OF POETRY (ELEMENTARY THROUGH HIGH SCHOOL)

SUMMARY: A stunning collection of poetry that begs to be read aloud. While the sheer span of the collection cannot help but trace the impressive growth of self-awareness and pride among African Americans, it is thrilling to hear not just echoes of hope and courage but an indomitable demand for freedom in even the earliest pieces (see Phyllis Wheatley's eighteenth century poems as one example). The collection is far ranging and powerful, with samples from 25 of America's finest poets, including Langston Hughes, Fenton Johnson, Jean Toomer, Gwendolyn Brooks, Maya Angelou, Nikki Giovanni, Alice Walker, and Rita Dove.

LESSON IDEA: Let your students do the reading, with some interpretation. Try choral reading, with individual groups each selecting one poem to perform for the class. At the end, bring in the traits of ideas and voice by talking about common themes and feelings that emerge through the poems. Despite vast spans in time between writings, these poems share many common threads. Why?

Cobb, Vicki. *Blood & Gore.* 1997. New York: Scholastic.
ISBN: 0-590-92665-9.

TECHNICAL PICTURE BOOK (ELEMENTARY THROUGH HIGH SCHOOL)

SUMMARY: This is well-illustrated, well-written technical information. It's clear, concise, and presented in short, well-connected sentences: "A drop of blood the size of a dot at the end of a sentence is packed with five million red blood cells. Each tiny red cell looks like a doughnut with a dent instead of a hole. Red cells are like tiny rafts floating through your body in a river of about five quarts of a straw-colored liquid called *plasma.*" This is the essence of good tech writing, and it's a good place to begin, even for older writers. Also use Cobb's book to show how to connect text to illustrations; she's a whiz.

LESSON IDEA: Share several of Cobb's pieces. Read them aloud and listen, but look, too. Put one or two on the overhead so you can study her style. Notice the sentence lengths; none are too long. None go on till you feel entangled or lost. Notice the connecting words and phrases also. See how they help you keep track of your thoughts? You can teach writers to imitate this simple style in two ways: (1) begin with some research information, and ask them to write it up in simple text, as if they were writing to students two to three years younger; or (2) (this is excellent for older students) begin with a slightly difficult techni-cal piece, and ask them to re-write it, simplifying it by making sentences slight-ly shorter and connecting ideas with good transitions. Good tech writing should leave the reader feeling smart-—like an insider. Can your students produce writing like that?

Duncan, David James. *River Teeth: Stories and Writings.* 1995. New York: Bantam. ISBN: 0-553-37827-9.

SHORT STORY/ESSAY ANTHOLOGY (HIGH SCHOOL)

SUMMARY: "Hours flew past, and birds" ("Her Idiots," p. 21). Not everyone can get by with a sentence like that. Duncan can because he writes with such ease, such grace that every line seems perfectly crafted. He demonstrates in his writing all the best that we tell students of fluency: variety, rhythm, structure. "Red Coats" is a classic. Do not miss it.

LESSON IDEA: Share "Red Coats" aloud—or invite one or two (or more) of your students to read it. Ask them to notice, *really* notice, the way Duncan weaves words into sentences. (Having some text to mark up is helpful in this analysis.) Discuss some of his techniques; how does he manage to work in so much variety in both length and structure? You may wish to extend the lesson by asking students to write a paragraph imitating his style, and using the "River Teeth" theme. Of course, you will need to talk about the meaning of this intriguing phrase: What exactly are "river teeth" and how do they connect to our lives? An excellent center point for any serious personal essay, as Duncan's introduction shows. Does the metaphor work for you?

 Fleischman, Paul. *Joyful Noise: Poems for Two Voices.* 1988. New York: HarperCollins. ISBN: 0-06021852-5.

VIC'S PICKS POETRY FORMATTED FOR READERS' THEATER (ELEMENTARY THROUGH HIGH SCHOOL)

SUMMARY: These poems are pre-formatted for two voices, and invite playful reading. All are about the insect world—some fairly serious, some quite funny. So they're good for developing voice, too. Students can alternate between individual readings and combined voices, giving them an opportunity to design their own fluent interpretations.

LESSON IDEA: Simply copy passages and provide time to rehearse! Follow-up: Invite students to create their own two-voice or multiple-voice poetry. This is a challenge, of course, but much less so once they've performed two or more of Fleischman's wonderful pieces.

See also

Fleischman, Paul. *I Am Phoenix: Poems for Two Voices.* (Same idea, but birds, rather than insects.)

Fox, Mem. *Night Noises*. Illustrated by Terry Denton. 1989. New York: Harcourt Brace. ISBN: 0-15-257421-2.

PICTURE BOOK (PRIMARY THROUGH MIDDLE SCHOOL)

SUMMARY: Lily Laceby is nearly ninety and lives in a cottage in the hills with Butch Aggie, her dog, as her only companion. One wild winter evening, snug and warm by the fire, Lily drifts off to sleep. As she dreams peacefully of bygone days, strange noises begin to echo in the night, alarming Butch Aggie. As the commotion grows louder, Butch Aggie leaps up to see who could be out and about—and what mischief they might be up to. The story is just suspenseful enough, and the illustrations cleverly depict the action. The most outstanding feature of the book is Mem Fox's marvelous word choice; verbs are particularly noteworthy.

LESSON IDEA: Ask students to listen for powerful words, and list their favorites. To extend this lesson, try this: Rewrite a portion of *Night Noises* using ordinary, boring verbs. Make the text large, with plenty of space to write. Underline your new, boring verbs. *Before reading the book aloud,* ask students to help you revise the story using *powerful* verbs. Write in students' suggestions using a felt pen. Include as many as you can make room for. (Younger students may need some preliminary help on what you mean by a <u>verb</u>.) When all suggestions are listed, go back through your text, and ask students to choose the *one* word they like best in each case. Circle it. Then, read Mem Fox's original and compare. **Extension:** Ask students to look at a piece of their own writing, and circle or underline any two words (verbs or others) they would like to change. They can work in pairs or groups to brainstorm options. Students should not feel compelled to make changes; this is a lesson on *exploring* different ways to say something.

Frost, Robert. *Versed in Country Things*. Poetry selected by Edward Connery Lathem. 1996. New York: Little, Brown and Company. ISBN: 0-8212-2288-0.

POETRY COLLECTION (MIDDLE SCHOOL, HIGH SCHOOL)

SUMMARY: Within these pages, you'll find some of Frost's less known pieces, every one a tribute to the country life of the New England he loved, each set off to perfection by the dramatic black and white photography of B. A. King.

LESSON IDEA: Choose some poems to read aloud, or ask students to be readers, perhaps in choral groups. Talk about the feelings these poems evoke in readers. How are those feelings enhanced by the photographs?

Extension: Ask students to write their own poems, free verse or with the subtle rhyme so characteristic of Frost. Students should feel free to complement their poetry with photographs or pictures of any kind (including original art, if they wish), and even to base a poem upon a piece of art. Sometimes it's easier if the art comes first!

Grimes, Nikki. *My Man Blue.* **Illustrated by Jerome Lagarrigue. 1999. New York: Penguin Putnam.** ISBN: **0-8037-2326-1.**

POETIC PICTURE BOOK (PRIMARY THROUGH HIGH SCHOOL)

SUMMARY: In this incredible story-poem, Grimes tells a story that has both depth and heart. A muscular, streetwise boxer with insight and an understanding of how life works befriends a young boy. One has lost a father, one a son; together, they help fill in the deep holes of loss, each for the other. Compassionate, beautiful, an inspired blend of street smarts and poetry.

LESSON IDEA: This book is a natural for interpretive reading, choral reading, or readers' theater. Invite students to choose a poem and do a small-group (three to four students) reading of that poem, "performing" it for the class. Encourage them to really think through the meanings of words and the feelings embedded within each line. Performing a number of poems together creates a strong sense of story as well as character. You'll find that the complexity of Grimes' language along with the unerring rhythms makes every poem a pleasure to share orally.

Sentence
Fluency
93

Hughes, Langston. *The Block.* **1995. Collage art by Romare Beardon (Copyright 1995 by the Metropolitan Museum of Art). New York: Viking.** ISBN: **0-670-86501-X.**

POETRY AND ART (MIDDLE SCHOOL, HIGH SCHOOL)

SUMMARY: The poetry in this book is stunning. Ditto Romare Beardon's amazing collages, in which you will find new meaning each time you look. Put the two together, and you have a powerful picture of life in Harlem from the inside out. You might begin by reading aloud "Theme for English B," and just asking students to react—perhaps write a note to the poet. Read it more than once; it bears second and third looks.

LESSON IDEA: Discuss the relationships of poetry and collage. One is auditory, one is visual. Yet, in many ways, they complement each other. Poetry/ collage combinations can be used in so many ways: to reflect the lives of

African Americans or people of other cultures, to reflect the lives of teenagers or students, to advertise an upcoming event or holiday, to celebrate the life of a famous person, to teach a concept. You might ask students to work in groups to create poetry/collage combinations that teach viewers/readers about children, other cultures, the elderly, physics, geometry, verbs, orangutans, fractions, rain-forests, themselves—or any subject at all.

See also

Myers, Walter Dean. *Harlem.* 1997. New York: Scholastic Press.
Art by Christopher Myers.

Equally rhythmic, with beautiful layout and text that sings itself right off the page and into your very soul.

Killgallon, Don and Jenny Killgallon. *Daily Sentence Composing.* 1999. Wilmington, MA: Great Source Education Group, Inc.

DAILY MINILESSONS WITH SENTENCE FORMS (MIDDLE SCHOOL)

SUMMARY: Anyone can come up with sentence drills or lessons. What's different about this book is that each lesson is based on wonderful examples from literature. Students work on major concepts such as chunking, unscrambling, sentence openers and closers, and combining—all with carefully selected models from the pros to guide them.

LESSON IDEA: Lessons are built in. It's just a question of how far you wish to go and which concepts you wish to emphasize. Don't forget now and then to take time to read sentences aloud; this is quite a collection.

(Gr 6) ISBN: 0-669-46936-X
(Gr 7) ISBN: 0-669-46937-8
(Gr 8) ISBN: 0-669-46939-4

Koscielniak, Bruce. *Hear, Hear, Mr. Shakespeare.* 1998. New York: Houghton Mifflin Company. ISBN: 0-395-87495-5.

PICTURE BOOK BASED ON THE WORKS OF WILLIAM SHAKESPEARE (MIDDLE SCHOOL, HIGH SCHOOL)

SUMMARY: Here's a clever book older reader-writers, especially fans of Shakespeare, will enjoy. It's brimming with lively quotations from the bard, each set relating to a specific theme, from acting to the weather. The lines quoted are always followed by the plays and scenes cited. It's a delight to explore the language or just to read the quotations aloud for their musical quality and rhythm.

LESSON IDEA: Collect quotations from a wide range of authors on a theme of your students' choice. You can create a bulletin board display on entertainment, violence, weather, travel—or whatever. For a more personalized approach, let students select individual topics and collect quotations to fit their topics; quotations do NOT have to come from Shakespeare or any famous author, though some could. They can also come from family and friends, as well as from your student authors themselves. The more diversely students think, the more widely appealing their collections will be.

Locker, Thomas. *Home*. 1998. New York: Harcourt Brace & Company. ISBN: 0-15-201473-X.

POETRY AND POETIC PROSE EXCERPTS (ELEMENTARY THROUGH HIGH SCHOOL)

SUMMARY: Through the voices of many well-known authors, from Robert Frost to Jane Yolen, we travel coast to coast, pausing here and there to ponder the meaning and the beauty of the places they call "home." Each piece can stand by itself, but together they describe a glorious journey not only across the country but to the center of our very selves.

LESSON IDEA: Choral reading is one obvious possibility here, and the common theme brought to life through such different voices makes these selections a delight to share aloud. Each has its own rhythm and beat, some more forceful and dynamic, some very quiet and speculative. There is much room for interpretation. They are short, so your students can read through a selection several times before presenting it. Some pieces, such as Robert Frost's "From Once By the Pacific" have such strong imagery that they invite discussion about the relationship of fluency to ideas. Can a writer literally push an image forward and into our minds through the rhythm of a sentence?

Locker, Thomas. *Water Dance*. 1997. New York: Harcourt Brace & Company. ISBN: 0-15-201284-2.

VIC'S PICKS

POETIC PICTURE BOOK (PRIMARY THROUGH HIGH SCHOOL)

SUMMARY: Water is the most common substance on earth. We ourselves are more than two-thirds water. And amazingly, the same amount of water has been cycling around our planet for millions of years—yet how much do we know of that cycle? This is a wonderfully informative book, done as poetry (as the title might suggest), and it's one of the finest books around for choral reading because the lines are so dramatic, the invitations to interpret meaning through dance or other movement so clear and open.

LESSON IDEA: Use this book to teach fluency through choral reading or readers' theater. It divides nicely into 13 parts, but you can readily adjust that to suit the size of your class, if you wish. Invite participants to use sound effects, multiple voices, singing, dance, gestures, or whatever feels right. Provide background music with water sounds, if you can. You'll enjoy this one.

Marsden, John. *Prayer for the twenty-first century.* 1998. New York: Star Bright Books. ISBN: 1-887734-42-2.

POETIC PICTURE BOOK (ELEMENTARY THROUGH HIGH SCHOOL)

SUMMARY: This isn't really a "picture book" in the usual sense. It's a work of art. Arrestingly, provocatively illustrated by a wide range of artists whose vision beautifully complements Marsden's poetic text. It takes only brief moments to read; it will haunt you for hours. Sometimes repetition *does* work; all rules in writing shatter in the hands of experts. (Despite the word "prayer," the book is religious only in the broadest spiritual sense; it is a book of hopes, wishes, and dreams.)

LESSON IDEA: Read the book aloud and invite students to create their own personal wishes, dreams, reflections for the century to come. What do they hope for? What do they envision? As they focus on the future, how often do they think of the past?

Sentence
Fluency
96

Milne, A. A. *The Pooh Story Book.* 1965. New York: E.P. Dutton. ISBN: 0-525-37546-5.

FICTIONAL CHAPTER BOOK (PRIMARY THROUGH HIGH SCHOOL)

SUMMARY: "It rained and it rained and it rained. Piglet told himself that never in his life, and *he* was goodness knows *how* old—three, was it, or four?—never had he seen so much rain. Days and days and days." Some of the most fluent writing ever, some of the best dialogue, some of the strongest imagery lies right within the covers of a book that for so many feels like an old friend—*The Pooh Story Book.* This edition features three of the best-loved Pooh tales, each a masterpiece of fluency. If you've not looked in on Pooh for a while, you'll be surprised how sophisticated the text really is, and how the words dance across the page. This is a book for all ages.

LESSON IDEA: Use this book to teach fluency through oral reading or readers' theater. There are no bad parts! Also use it to illustrate the power of good, natural dialogue in conveying feelings and ideas. Notice the conventions, too: When does Milne use capitals?

Morrison, Toni with Slade Morrison. *The Big Box.*
Illustrated by Giselle Potter. 1999. New York: Hyperion
Books for Children. ISBN: 0-7868-0416-5.

PICTURE BOOK (PRIMARY THROUGH HIGH SCHOOL)

SUMMARY: Simply magnificent. This is Pulitzer Prize winner Toni
Morrison's first book for younger readers (inspired by a story first invented by
her son Slade at the age of nine), and it will captivate young and older readers
alike. What do we do with people when their behavior makes us "nervous"?
According to Morrison, we put them in a box. It's a "big box," but it's not big
enough. Though it can hold all sorts of material things with which we appease
them, it cannot contain the thing most precious of all: freedom. This is surely a
book to use in teaching ideas, voice, and word choice, but its poetic, lyrical
style makes it a gem for fluency. Giselle Potter's illustrations capture the
essence of Morrison's gently stated but biting message perfectly. Children who
have ever felt misunderstood by adults or entrapped by adult rules will identify
at once. A book you'll want to read again and again, to yourself and to others.

LESSON IDEA: This book simply cries out for choral reading or readers' theater. Its profound and insightful message invites interpretive reading, and because
the message is delivered through multiple voices, from multiple points of view, the
readings will have texture and interest. Try it and see; you'll feel you're putting on
a play (for you are). Morrison's text is as satisfying as a full-course meal.

Sentence
Fluency
97

Myers, Walter Dean. *Slam!* **1996. New York: Scholastic Press.**
ISBN: 0-590-48667-5.

YOUNG ADULT NOVEL (MIDDLE SCHOOL, HIGH SCHOOL)

SUMMARY: Slam tells us, "I got the moves, the eye, and the heart. You can
take my game to the bank and wait around for the interest." You can believe
him. You can also enjoy the way he talks, for it's much like the way he plays
the game: With a beat. With style. With the moves. This is a gritty, realistic
coming-of-age story about a young black, talented athlete making his way on
the streets and basketball courts of Harlem. And sometimes, it is only the basketball that keeps him going. It's realistic without being gratuitous in violence
or rough language. Outstanding characterization and a beautiful example of the
power of first-person narrative.

LESSON IDEA: Ask students to try just a short piece of first-person narrative, trying to capture the rhythm and flow of the way they talk. It has to sound
natural—not too formal, but not overdone, either. First-person writing is a little
like having a conversation with yourself. An excellent foundation for personal
essay writing, which adds just a pinch of formality.

Nye, Naomi Shihab, selector of poems and artwork. *The Space Between Our Footsteps: Poems and Paintings from the Middle East.* 1998. New York: Simon and Schuster. ISBN: 0-689-81233-7.

POETRY AND ART (MIDDLE SCHOOL, HIGH SCHOOL)

SUMMARY: More than 100 poets and artists of the Middle East contributed their unique skills and perspectives to this beautiful collection, an exploration of another culture. Between the art and the poetry, you will gain a glimpse— just a glimpse—of these philosophical people. The meaning that lies "between the footsteps."

LESSON IDEA: These are not simple poems. They take thought. You may wish to read them aloud, but also provide copies for students to explore, mark, and respond to. Think about asking students to choose one poem each and analyze the tone and meaning through their personal response. What overall impressions emerge? Do you find common themes? Are certain meanings "between the footsteps" hard to reach? Ask students to read poems aloud to demonstrate the remarkable fluency, then to lead a discussion on what the poems and/or art reveal about the philosophy and perspective of the people who created them.

Paulsen, Gary. *Dogteam.* Illustrated by Ruth Wright Paulsen. 1993. New York: Bantam Doubleday Dell Publishing Group, Inc. ISBN: 0-385-30550-8.

POETIC PICTURE BOOK (PRIMARY THROUGH HIGH SCHOOL)

SUMMARY: For sheer poetry, this book is hard to beat. Like the dog team it celebrates, Paulsen's musical text dances "through the trees, in and out" and right into our hearts. So beautiful, so engaging is this book in text, in rhythm, in illustration, it will beckon you to jump right on the sled and run, run right into the night with the team, to join the "dogdance" in the "dogcold" and "dognight." A book by and for people who love dogs and love the unique beauty of the northern Minnesota nights.

LESSON IDEA: This book is ideal for choral reading—even for quite young readers (say grades 2–3). You can divide the book into six to thirteen parts, ideally with about three to four students in a group. You can combine two classes for this activity, if necessary. Give students time to rehearse segments for reading aloud in single, double, or multiple voices (or a mix of all three). Let them know that in choral reading they can be imaginative, varying patterns, volume, and numbers of voices as they go; and as they do so, they will be thinking of fluency and inflection, interpreting text through sound. The idea with choral reading is to make the audience *feel and experience* the text, not just hear it like a song on the radio. If you have some soft music with outdoor sound effects (loons, geese, coyotes, wolves, waterfalls), you may wish to play this before or during the reading. It adds a lot!

Rigamonti, Justin. *The Pigs Went Marching Out!* 1998. Kansas City, MO: Landmark Editions, Inc. ISBN: 0-933849-70-2.

PICTURE BOOK (PRIMARY THROUGH HIGH SCHOOL)

SUMMARY: This wonderfully rhythmic, humorous tale of a rebellious pig and his not too bright cohorts will delight younger children—but it may inspire older students to become writers themselves. Landmark, you see, publishes books by young writers (contest winners), and Justin was just 17 when he wrote and illustrated this book. Many other titles are available; address and phone number are provided for prospective young authors.

LESSON IDEA: With younger students, simply have fun reading the rhythmic text aloud. You may wish to get up and march to the beat—or even encourage students to echo some of the lines or to clap to the rhythm. They will feel it! With older students, use the book as a model. Talk about why it works as a children's book and why it might have been selected as a contest winner. If you like, encourage students to try their hand at writing a short children's book, fiction or nonfiction. Talk about what's essential: the right voice and tone, the right words, an interesting topic, and so on. If you like, let students work in pairs, so one may focus on illustrating, one on writing and editing.

Sentence
Fluency
99

Sagan, Carl. *Cosmos.* 1980. New York: Random House. ISBN: 0-394-50294-9.

VIC'S PICKS **NONFICTION CHAPTER BOOK ON ASTRONOMY** (MIDDLE SCHOOL, HIGH SCHOOL)

SUMMARY: "Human beings grew up in forests. We have a natural affinity for them. How lovely a tree is, straining toward the sky. Its leaves harvest sunlight to photosynthesize, so trees compete by shadowing their neighbors. If you look closely, you can often see two trees pushing and shoving with languid grace." (*Cosmos,* p. 33) This is one of the great books ever. It isn't often we get an opportunity to get inside the mind of a person who thinks like a poet and a scientist at the same time.

LESSON IDEA: Select passages to read aloud—or reprint some and ask students to read them aloud. Analyze them for fluency (look especially at sentence beginnings) and even try some restructuring; many of Sagan's paragraphs can be reformatted as poetry. Try it! Imitation is a greatest way to learn voice, fluency—any trait. Pull a piece from a biology, physics, or chemistry textbook and re-do it in Sagan's style. Extend the challenge by bringing Sagan's voice into another context entirely. For instance, imagine him doing a review of a film or local restaurant—or a summary of how to improve science education in the schools. Write a letter, as Sagan, to the author(s) of any science book; exchange letters and have the "authors" write back!

San Francisco WritersCorps, editors. *What It Took for Me to Get Here.*

POEMS AND VIGNETTES BY STUDENTS (MIDDLE SCHOOL, HIGH SCHOOL)

SUMMARY: You will be swept away by the strength, the force, the music that shimmers in these lines. Sometimes raw, sometimes tender, these poems and stories trace the feelings and blossoming thoughts of young writers. Use them to teach not only fluency, but ideas and voice, too. Young writers put their voices together and created a chorus of passion and life.

LESSON IDEA: Read the poems aloud. Perform them. Imitate them. Do choral readings or read-arounds. You cannot go wrong. Many beg for a readers' theater approach, for there is so much meaning embedded in this text, it's hard for a single voice to bring it all out. This book is a lesson in freeing the voice—letting go. What results is the fluency of the river when the dam bursts.

Sentence Fluency 100

Dr. Seuss and Jack Prelutsky. *Hooray for Diffendoofer Day!* Illustrated by Lane Smith. 1998. New York: Random House. ISBN: 0-679-89008-4.

POETIC PICTURE BOOK (PRIMARY THROUGH HIGH SCHOOL)

SUMMARY: A zany look at the world of testing and how it throws everyone into a dither. A wonderfully perceptive yet fun to read aloud book. Good therapy for those seriously involved in testing!

LESSON IDEA: This book is readily adaptable to choral reading—and students have fun with it because the word play is bizarre and whimsical, and the rhythm is right on. So often, rhyming poetry doesn't work because the writer doesn't really have an ear for rhythm. This one works, and students enjoy playing different parts. Older students will also enjoy the appendix: How the book came to be. It's a lesson on revision and cooperative writing.

Books
for Teaching

Conventions and Creative Layout

Conventions include anything a copy editor would deal with: spelling, punctuation, grammar and usage, paragraphing, and capitalization. We have expanded the definition slightly to also include issues of layout: how text is presented on the page, whether for a business letter, poster, brochure, advertisement, or whatever. With so much emphasis on conventional correctness in twenty-first century assessment, it is important to help students learn conventions in a way that is both simple and pleasurable. We believe this collection provides some of the finest models for conventions and layout, and also encourages the rigorous teaching of editing without ever making a potentially grim topic dull.

Teach conventions fluency by

- Saving faulty samples of text and asking students to hunt for errors
- Providing punctuation-free text and having students fill in the punctuation as you read aloud
- Practicing editing and layout—individually and in groups
- Identifying conventions and copy editor's symbols (younger students)
- Using copy editor's symbols (older students)
- Analyzing samples of creative layout

Conventions
101

Bunting, Eve. *Your Move*. Illustrated by James Ransome. 1998. New York: Harcourt Brace. ISBN: 0-15-200181-6.

PICTURE BOOK (MIDDLE SCHOOL)

SUMMARY: This is a very powerful book, and when you first read it, you may say to yourself, "Why is it listed with *conventions*? Why not ideas—voice—fluency—word choice?" It *is* strong in virtually all categories. It holds an important message and delivers it with punch. It also holds students' attention. The realism of the characters, their life circumstances, and their dialogue gives it authenticity. Also look, though, at the extraordinarily creative use of punctuation and other conventions (e.g., paragraphing) to create a book based mostly on dialogue. Students often want to write dialogue; they do not always know conventionally how to set it up. This little picture book will show them.

LESSON IDEA: Teaching and assessing are among the best ways to learn, as we know. This lesson gives students an opportunity to teach and assess conventions. You will model first, though. Make up two or three multiple-choice questions based on the book. Here's one example (taken from the book):

In the following example, what mark of punctuation would work best after the word *jacket*?

> I hand him my jacket "Hold this."

a) a period
b) a comma
c) a question mark
d) nothing

Answer: a) a period. Why? Because the sample is really two sentences.

Now comes the fun part. Ask students to work in pairs and to come up with *three* questions per pair based on Eve Bunting's text. They should base their questions on the text, but they do not have to *quote* her text in the questions. For instance, one question might be, "What mark of punctuation do you use to indicate that a person is speaking?" Ask them to be creative and to hunt for conventional items that are useful—but also interesting. Let them know that you need to approve the questions for clarity and correctness. Then, give one set of questions each day to the class for a mini-lesson on conventions. The test item writers must be prepared to explain why their answer is correct and the others are not. When everyone has finished presenting, talk about the relationship between conventions and meaning. **Note**: Depending on students' ability level, you can use almost *any* text from the simplest of picture books to the most complex technical writing to create a lesson like this. This Eve Bunting book is particularly rich in its use of conventions, however, and offers opportunities to generate a wide range of questions.

Cappon, Rene J. *Associated Press Guide to News Writing: A Handbook for Writers from America's Leading News Service.* 1991. New York: Prentice Hall. ISBN: 0-13-053679-2.

HOW-TO TEXT FOR NEWS WRITING (HIGH SCHOOL)

SUMMARY: A *great* little book that handles not only conventions nicely, but also issues of tone and style, wordiness, avoiding jargon, keeping it concise, and so much more—all from a newsworthy perspective. Use this book to help students develop a strong sense of what good nonfiction writing is all about without killing voice. News stories aren't novels. But they aren't the encyclopedia either.

LESSON IDEA: Do several minilessons based on ideas from the book. You might work on appropriate tone, good leads, avoiding wordiness, or whatever. Then, pull several short articles from the local paper and score them on one, two or three traits connected to what you've been studying. Talk about what you could do to improve them. **Extension:** Ask students to create faulty news stories, containing a few conventional errors plus one or two other problems. Make the print big; double space. Now trade stories and play editor. See what partners can do to improve the stories.

Eldon, Kathy, ed. *The Journey Is the Destination: The Journals of Dan Eldon.* 1997. San Francisco: Chronicle Books. ISBN: 0-8118-1586-2.

PHOTOGRAPHIC JOURNAL (HIGH SCHOOL)

SUMMARY: Dan Eldon, a Reuters photographer, was stoned to death at the age of 22 in Somalia in July 1993. Eldon was killed by a mob reacting to the United Nations' bombing raid on the suspected headquarters of General Mohammed Farah Aidid. Prior to his death, Eldon, a student of music and art, created through his extraordinary photography a world of unbelievable depth, imagery, symbolism, and amazing visual connections. To anyone interested in visual journalism, this book is a must-have piece of art. It captures at once the joy and danger, the sickness and hope and sheer fun of life as Dan saw it through his artist's eyes. It is a visual diary, a rare journey, and it will leave you saying, "My word—what if this talented, visionary spirit had lived to see 60? What wonders—what truths about ourselves—might he have shown us?"

He is the photographic counterpart of Carl Sagan, a rare mind, but taking us more within than without. A feast for the eyes and spirit you won't forget.

LESSON IDEA: Put your "photo journalists" to work creating a wordless story on "A day in the life of . . ." *anyone* at all: student, teacher, police officer, business person, parent, dog, tree; use your collective imaginations. Students can actually take color or black and white photos if this resource is available, or they can use sketches or pictures from magazines. Make sure they look carefully through Eldon's book first, along with any others your library may contain with a similar format. Discover the power of saying it without words, when layout is ALL.

Hesse, Karen. *The Music of Dolphins.* 1996. New York: Scholastic. ISBN: 0-590-89798-5.

VIC'S PICKS YOUNG ADULT NOVEL (ELEMENTARY THROUGH HIGH SCHOOL)

SUMMARY: This is an intriguing young adult novel about a girl, Mila, who literally lives with dolphins and identifies with them. Raised by dolphins from the age of four till fourteen, she reluctantly returns to the world of humans, where she becomes the relentless focus of researchers who care more about studying her than helping her. What is fascinating is the way Hesse uses font style and size to reflect changes in Mila's thinking—and her understanding and identification with the world around her. It is almost like tracing the language development of a young child. An intriguing story, cleverly formatted.

LESSON IDEA: First, discuss how conventions change within the book and why. What is the author telling us by changing the font? What is the relationship between conventions and meaning (ideas)? **Extension:** Ask students to create a dialogue in which conventions play a central role because they enhance meaning or mood or show something about the characters. Talk about conventions you can play with: font size, italics, ellipses, exclamation points, capital letters, quotation marks, etc. What might their use or lack of use show? Share writing in small groups to show various ways students find to use conventions to reveal mood, tone, or a character's way of thinking.

Kiester, Jane Bell. *Caught'Ya Again! More Grammar With a Giggle.* 1992. Gainesville, FL: Maupin House. ISBN: 0-929895-09-6.

TEXT WITH PRACTICE LESSONS FOR EDITING (PRIMARY THROUGH HIGH SCHOOL)

SUMMARY: Similar in philosophy and format to Jane's earlier, widely acclaimed book, but this time with all-new stories and sentences, and editing practice even for second graders. As with the earlier book, lessons are lively, engaging, and short. It's easy to work this into your current curriculum, and students will benefit from the excellent practice.

LESSON IDEA: Everything you need is provided within the book.

Kiester, Jane Bell. *Caught'Ya! Grammar with a Giggle.* 1990. Gainesville, FL: Maupin House. ISBN: 0-929895-04-5.

TEXT WITH PRACTICE LESSONS FOR EDITING (ELEMENTARY THROUGH HIGH SCHOOL)

SUMMARY: Teacher Jane Bell Kiester makes the teaching of editing both fun and rewarding in her no-fail method that allows all students—even those who feel very challenged as editors—to experience success. Her lessons take about ten minutes per day, and are taken from the text of appealing, grade-level based stories. Students "catch" errors, either on their own, or during class editing practice; either way, they receive credit.

LESSON IDEA: Everything you need is provided within the book. You need only copy sentences onto a chalkboard or overhead—and let the editing party begin!

Lasky, Kathryn. *The Most Beautiful Roof in the World: Exploring the Rainforest Canopy.* Photographs by Christopher G. Knight. 1997. New York: Harcourt, Brace & Company. ISBN: 0-15-200897-7.

NONFICTION PICTURE BOOK (MIDDLE SCHOOL, HIGH SCHOOL)

SUMMARY: Highly readable, informative, and a prize winner. The layout is striking, for the pictures are not just used as filler, but really enhance the text. Look through and imagine each photograph chosen with care: Ask yourself (and your students), "Out of perhaps a dozen possibilities, why did they choose this one? What makes it special?"

LESSON IDEA: Read a passage or two aloud, and ask students what they picture in their minds—or what they would like to see. *Then,* share Christopher G. Knight's outstanding photographs and compare expectations to reality. How much do the photographs add to the overall informational value? **Extension:** For the next piece of research writing, encourage students to use illustrations— original photographs, sketches, or excerpts from magazines, etc. Also ask them to do a short reflective piece on why they chose the illustrations they did and what they feel illustrations add to a text. Why is ours such a visual society? Discussion: Do we "read" pictures in the way we "read" text?

Layton, Marcia. *The Complete Idiot's Guide to Terrific Business Writing.* 1996. New York: Macmillan Publishing. ISBN: 0-02-861097-0.

HOW-TO TEXTBOOK ON BUSINESS WRITING (HIGH SCHOOL)

SUMMARY: It's a little arbitrary to list this with conventions because really, it's much broader in scope than that—but it does a whiz-bang job of showing the formalities of setting up a letter properly. In addition, though, it deals with important issues such as cutting to the chase, analyzing audience, breaking through writer's block, ensuring that your style matches the situation, and so on. It's up to date, too: e-mail, memos, press releases, and proposals are all included. Look for good tips on editing and polishing text also. Concise, useful, never dull.

LESSON IDEA: Instead of all writing the same letter, why not ask students to do a little role playing? You can let them choose their roles, or put a list of names and tasks in a basket (you and your students can invent these together) and have them draw: Oprah Winfrey writes a letter of complaint to her producer stating that too many commercials disrupt the flow of the program; Michael Jordan writes a letter of proposal to Nike attempting to sell a new product he has just developed; a member of the New York Times e-mails the President commenting on how dull press conferences have been of late; the President replies—and then sketches out notes for a press conference; the president of NBC drafts a note to the Board of Directors asking them to consider whether the network runs too many situation comedies; a local person writes to a news station complaining that the news is too violent and disturbing for her children to watch; the network responds to her complaint. The more diverse and inventive your situations, the more challenging and interesting your letters. Make the letters and other correspondence as interactive as you can by encouraging students to write to one another, then reply. As you go along, talk about what makes business correspondence effective. **Extension:** Create your own class rubric for good business writing.

Lederer, Richard. *Anguished English.* 1987. Charleston, SC: Wyrick and Company. ISBN: 0-941711-04-8.

VIC'S PICKS

COMPILATION OF HILARIOUS BLOOPERS FROM CHILDREN'S AND ADULT'S WRITING (PRIMARY THROUGH HIGH SCHOOL, IF YOU'RE SELECTIVE)

SUMMARY: You don't have to use this book in teaching to love it. You can just curl up with it on a rainy afternoon to cheer yourself up. But suppose you do wish to teach editing skills. What's more fun to edit than the bloopers of others: e.g., "A virtuoso is a musician with real high morals" (p. 4). What was the writer thinking when he/she wrote this? We all do it sooner or later; maybe that's what makes us laugh.

LESSON IDEA: Choose a few favorites, focusing on sentence sense, misuse of words, "original spelling," or a mix. Let students have some fun editing text that will give them a laugh as they work.

Monceaux, Morgan. *Jazz: My Music, My People*. 1994. New York: Random House. ISBN: 0-679-85618-8.

BIOGRAPHICAL SKETCHES WITH ARTISTIC LAYOUT (MIDDLE SCHOOL, HIGH SCHOOL)

SUMMARY: Here's an example of informational text as art. It's a whole collection of research papers with a common theme: the greatest jazz musicians of all time. Each is represented visually through an artistic rendering that combines painting and wrap-around text; and the life of each is summarized in lively, snappy prose that has just the right voice for informational writing on a semi-technical topic. You don't have to be a musician to appreciate the details, but if you know blues from jazz—if you know what a "run" is, it helps. Each biography has voice and heart, a true feeling of reverence for the gifted person it portrays; and it invites the reader to be an insider, too. Pull up a chair, have a listen. You'll like it. This is highly skillful layout, too. The wrap-around text is a striking innovation—one you may wish to imitate in your students' own research writings. Who says a research collection has to look dry and dull?

LESSON IDEA: Invite students to do biographies or autobiographies by first sketching the person (they can choose themselves!), then wrapping the text around the sketch, for a different look.

VIC'S PICKS

Strunk, William Jr. and E. B. White. *The Elements of Style, 4th edition*. 1999. Needham Heights, MA Allyn & Bacon. ISBN: 0-205-30902-X.

HOW-TO BOOK ON WRITING (MIDDLE AND HIGH SCHOOL)

SUMMARY: Among the best around, no writer's or editor's bookshelf should be without it. Only runs 85 pages, so you can read it annually, and it's good enough that you'll feel refreshed, not bored. It's packed with tips on writing correctly, yet with flourish. You needn't be dull to be formal and correct. You needn't be wordy to say a lot, either—and these authors are anything but. They "omit needless words," "avoid successions of long, loose sentences," and in general, heed their own excellent advice from start to finish.

LESSON IDEA: As you go through the year, create your own "Elements of Style" book, inviting each student to make one contribution. This could be a mini-lesson, brief quiz, piece of advice on writing well, tip for editing or revision, list of hot topics—or anything other young writers can use. At the end of the year, copy the complete book for students and/or add it to your library collection. Call it "Student to Student"—or something similar.

Volavkova, Hana, ed. . . . *I never saw another butterfly . . . Children's Drawings and Poems From Terezin Concentration Camp, 1942–1944.* 1993. New York: Schocken Books. ISBN: 0-8052-1015-6.

COLLECTION OF WRITINGS AND DRAWINGS (MIDDLE AND HIGH SCHOOL)

SUMMARY: One of the most haunting and powerful books of all time, combining hope and heartache. To say this work has voice is far too understated. It *is* voice. It *is* soul. From unspeakable horror comes poetry and prose so moving we can scarcely bear to read it—we have to take it in doses, a little at a time. As you go through the book, take a moment to reflect on how the authors and editors combined pictures and text, not always meant originally to go together (because they were created by different people), and how they used the space, sometimes crowding things together, sometimes creating a sense of openness. Beautifully done.

LESSON IDEA: In the real world of publication, authors and illustrators are rarely the same person. Next time your class works on any theme, whether it be the Holocaust, Civil War, recycling, or whatever, let some students be authors, some illustrators. Encourage teams to work together from the start so each can reinforce the other's meaning. Next time around, reverse roles.

Wilks, Mike. *Metamorphosis: the Ultimate Spot-the-Difference Book.* 1997. New York: Penguin Books. ISBN: 0-670-87666-6.

INTERACTIVE PICTURE/TEXT BOOK (MIDDLE AND HIGH SCHOOL)

SUMMARY: Here's an unusual book, highly interactive, that students enjoy immensely. Each page is printed twice; some are images, some text. Between versions 1 and 2, throughout the book, 250 changes have been made in various images, about 75 within the text. The question is, do you have a sharp enough eye to spot them?

LESSON IDEA: The format of this exceptional book has all lessons built right in. Students simply peruse pages, looking for differences between version one and version two; it's an ideal lesson for helping develop a proofreader's eye, which every writer needs. Plus, it's fun! Students see it as a game, not work. **Extension:** When students get really good, they can invent their own "metamorphosis" pieces, making small changes, then exchanging with partners to see who can spot changes most easily. Hint: To make this lesson successful, you will need to (1) keep samples short, (2) limit the number of changes, and (3) encourage students to insert mistakes in version 1, corrections in version 2! Have fun!

Teacher Resources

This collection of books takes a broad view of writing and writing instruction. It includes books that can help you improve your own writing skills, some designed to help you teach more effectively, and many intended to give you an in-depth understanding of writing process and good classroom practice. Within, you will find books that explore issues of setting up a writer's workshop, conferring with students effectively, using your own writing to model effective writing practice, understanding and teaching revision and editing, and weaving the six-trait model into your instruction. These books have been chosen because they provide intelligent, thoughtful discussions of timely, complex topics, and because they are conversational in style and therefore user friendly. Come in . . . browse!

Aronie, Nancy Slonim. *Writing From the Heart: Tapping the Power of Your Inner Voice.* **1998. New York: Hyperion.** ISBN: **0-7868-8287-5.**

SUMMARY: As Aronie tells us, "Every week ten people arrive in my workshop tentative and terrified, and four short days later, ten people leave empowered and ecstatic" (p. 123). You too will feel empowered by this extraordinary little book that shows how to use our own thoughts and feelings to create personal writing that is both moving and satisfying. Aronie is particularly good on the topics of listening, overcoming fear, or what she calls "melting the ice," using intuition and tapping into those parts of our lives no one else can experience unless we let them in through our writing. Her startling honesty speaks right to us, and is often blatantly funny. Each chapter closes with engaging, highly original exercises you can use to expand your own writing skills; you'll find yourself wanting to take some into secondary classrooms, too.

VIC'S PICKS

Ballenger, Bruce. *The Curious Researcher: A Guide to Writing Research Papers.* **1993. Needham Heights, MA: Allyn & Bacon.** ISBN: **0-205-29702-1.**

SUMMARY: "You probably think the words *research paper* and *interesting* are mutually exclusive." Ballenger's words show how well he understands how students—and many teachers—think about research. In this lively, entertaining book, he brings the world of research to life, showing the joy of digging for good information, trimming it down and shaping it to fit format and audience, finding the voice that is right for the context, using tables, revising for detail and word choice—and so much more. You *won't* find yourself yawning. Excellent sections on citing sources correctly (with examples), using the Internet (without overusing it) and taking good notes. Sample papers help students see what works and what doesn't. Though it's primarily directed at secondary, don't be without it from grade 6 on up if you teach research writing.

Bishop, Stephen, ed. *Songs in the Rough: From Heartbreak Hotel to Higher Love, Rock's Greatest Songs in Rough-Draft Form.* 1996. New York: St. Martin's Press. ISBN: 0-312-14048-7.

SUMMARY: Song writers from Elton John to the Beatles, Woodie Guthrie, Gene Pitney, Stevie Wonder, Bette Midler and Fleetwood Mac—to mention only a few—began many of their musical masterpieces via lyrics scrawled on the backs of airline tickets, menus, scraps of notebook paper, envelopes, or other humble writing media. This is a book celebrating the non-elegance of the rough draft and the remarkable journey of change along which writers, including song writers, travel on their way to meaning and satisfaction. Middle and high school students, many of whom are oldies fans, love browsing through this book to compare the originals to the finals that they know, and to see the kinds of changes writers make, from tiny editorial tweakings to major overhauls that barely left an original lyric intact (note Irene Cara's "Fame," p. 102).

Blake, Gary and Robert W. Bly. *The Elements of Technical Writing.* 1993. New York: Macmillan. ISBN: 0-02-013085-6.

SUMMARY: Blake and Bly write with ease and grace about the world of technical writing, from proposals and reports to letters, memos, and directions. They give wonderfully readable, practical advice on the importance of technical accuracy and clarity, ways of organizing technical information, keeping word choice simple, holding the attention of an audience, and using conventions with both skill and formality (with more than a few links to the six traits). Little nit picky things on uses of symbols, equations, numbers, graphics, etc., are also covered nicely. Many presentations are so well organized and complete that they can readily be translated into mini lessons or short self-informational (*How much do I know about this*?) quizzes for your students. While the content is more applicable to secondary students, teachers at *all* grade levels who deal with tech writing should consider this excellent little book.

Burdett, Lois. *Shakespeare Can Be Fun Series.* Willowdale, Ontario and Buffalo, NY: Firefly Books. ISBN: numbers listed below by title.

SUMMARY: Get ready to take the lid off all expectations for what younger students can do. In this incredible collection of student work, combined with her own ingenious rendering of Shakespeare's plays in rhyming couplets (works of art in themselves), Lois Burdett shows us that learning about Shakespeare can indeed be fun, inspiring, and educational. In her classroom,

Burdett encourages her second and third graders not only to listen to Shakespeare's plays, but to act them out, in costume. They "become" the characters, and in character, write each other notes and letters, as well as keeping journals, making maps, writing job application letters, and so forth. Through this process, their voice, mastery of word choice, and sentence fluency grow in breathtaking leaps. What they learn, they share in their writings and their art, which is amply and artfully exhibited in Burdett's books, each one a rare treat for the eye, ear, and heart.

- *A Child's Portrait of Shakespeare* ISBN: 0-88753-261-6
- *Macbeth for Kids* ISBN: 0-88753-279-9
- *A Midsummer Night's Dream for Kids* ISBN: 1-55209-124-4
- *Romeo and Juliet for Kids* ISBN: 1-55209-229-1
- *The Tempest for Kids* ISBN: 1-55209-326-3
- *Twelfth Night for Kids* ISBN: 0-88753-233-0

Burke, Jim. *The English Teacher's Companion: A Complete Guide to Classroom, Curriculum, and the Profession.* 1999. Portsmouth, NH: Greenwood-Heinemann. ISBN: 0-86709-475-3.

SUMMARY: Jim Burke is a teacher's teacher, and shares so much information and insight within this book you'll wonder how you ever did without it. It is impossible to list the many topics he discusses, but here's just a handful: Teaching reading, putting grammar in its rightful place, teaching writing, teaching speaking and listening, composing curriculum, helping students achieve media literacy, helping students with special needs find success, getting through your time as the "new teacher" on the block, and learning to enjoy parent-teacher conferences (no kidding—Jim will show you how). He literally takes you by the hand and walks you into the world of teaching.

Calkins, Lucy McCormick. *The Art of Teaching Writing, 2nd edition.* 1994. Portsmouth, NH: Heinemann. ISBN: 0-435-08817-3.

SUMMARY: A fundamental primer on teaching writing effectively, thoroughly, and with heightened sensitivity. It's long—and huge (you can build real muscle lifting it)—but it's highly readable, beautifully illustrated, and filled with carefully chosen student samples. Clearly, Calkins believes in letting students be our teachers. She is especially eloquent on the topics of developing a learning community, conferring effectively with students (and not assuming ownership of the writing), using literature, and teaching editing. Calkins achieves an effective balance between letting students thrive on their own and stepping in at the right moment to coach just enough. Even if you own the first edition, you'll find many new components added here, including a section on assessment.

Claggett, Fran, Louann Reid and Ruth Vinz. *The Daybooks of Critical Reading and Writing*. 1999. Wilmington, MA: Great Source Education Group (division of Houghton Mifflin). ISBNs by grade levels:

0-669-46440-6 (Gr 6)	0-669-46432-5 (Gr 10)
0-669-46443-0 (Gr 7)	0-669-46434-1 (Gr 11)
0-669-46444-9 (Gr 8)	0-669-46435-X (Gr 12)
0-669-46431-7 (Gr 9)	

GRADE LEVELS: 6 THROUGH 12 (READING/WRITING COLLECTIONS IN INTERACTIVE JOURNAL FORMAT)

SUMMARY: The *Daybooks* are absolutely unlike anything else for building the bridge between reading and writing skills. First, they are interactive journals, *not* anthologies. Second, they include a stunning span of writing, from poetry and fiction to the finest nonfiction, informational writing and persuasive essays around. Collections range from traditional to very modern, with something to catch every student's ear. Both reluctant reader/writers and those who routinely probe the depths will find lessons to challenge but allow for success. All samples are carefully chosen *short* excerpts—sometimes several on a single theme—interwoven with highly creative writing activities that invite students to record thoughts, assess professional work, sound off, create their own imitative versions, and use other authors' work as a launching point for their own writings. Yes, students DO write in the books; the layout is enticing and the whole so rich, complete and diverse, it is like a verbal rainforest.

Claggett, Fran. *A Measure of Success*. 1995. Portsmouth, NH: Greenwood-Heinemann. ISBN: 0-86709-373-0.

SUMMARY: Fran begins her book with these important words: "Teachers are engaged in assessment every minute they are in the classroom" (p. 1). Throughout this enlightening book, she never loses sight of the ongoing nature of assessment, and the many forms it can take. She insists that we begin by defining our subject. Whether dealing with reading or writing, how do we assess well if we don't know what it is we're looking for? This book offers a common sense approach to framing assessment by assigning work that will actually elicit the student responses we're after, and—this is emphasized throughout—*always* making students a part of the assessment process, through reflective reading, discussion, checklists, creation of rubrics, and portfolio assessment. A large portion of the book is dedicated to portfolios, as Fran encourages us to take a panoramic view of student performance. Numerous examples of student work, checklists, and rubrics invite us to think carefully about what we assess and how.

Collins, James L. *Strategies for Struggling Writers*. 1998. New York: Guilford Press. ISBN: 1-57230-299-2.

SUMMARY: This sensitive book thoughtfully blends the best of writing process with more direct strategies that truly help struggling writers get past the blank page. Collins combines his research findings with numerous real life examples to illustrate the power of talking aloud, visualizing and using graphics, drawing, borrowing and even "copying" in your own words (no, it isn't cheating—that's just our conditioning), imitation, making the most of modeling, providing students with simple, easy-to-follow rubrics, and much more. The book is packed with practical advice you can use to help your challenged writers find success in a writing workshop. Adaptable to virtually all grade levels.

Countryman, Joan. *Writing to Learn Mathematics: Strategies That Work, K–12*. 1992. Portsmouth, NH: Heinemann. ISBN: 0-435-08329-5.

SUMMARY: Looking for a way to weave math and writing together? Look no further. From journal entries to research papers, Joan Countryman will show you how to turn math into one of the most intriguing topics around. As students write—and *think*—mathematically, they not only learn to organize with care and to use words with precision, they also learn to reason and reflect. Math teachers can go a long way in making tech writing a natural part of the curriculum. This extraordinary little book lights the way.

Fletcher, Ralph and Joann Portalupi. *Craft Lessons: Teaching Writing K–8*. 1998. New York: Stenhouse Publishers. ISBN: 1-57110-073-3.

VIC'S PICKS

SUMMARY: Virtually every lesson in this book connects to some trait or other: e.g., *Deciding Where to Begin* (organization), *Finding a Focus* (ideas), *The Give-Away Lead* (organization), *Unpacking a Heavy Sentence* (fluency), *Using Stronger Verbs* (word choice). Probably the authors did not set out to write a "trait" book; yet because the traits *are* the core of good writing, the link follows naturally. The lessons, like their titles, are clever, and offer numerous engaging approaches to developing important writing skills. Nearly all are connected to one or more pieces of literature, and the authors are very explicit in suggesting how to use the literature to launch a lesson. The lessons support writers' workshop, offering a repertoire of writing approaches an author can use to draft or revise. Lessons run just one page each, and are neatly arranged by Grade levels: K–2, 3–4, and 5–8. Leans toward creative writing.

Fox, Mem. *Radical Reflections: Passionate Opinions on Teaching, Learning, and Living.* **1993. New York: Harcourt Brace & Company. ISBN: 0-15-607947-X.**

SUMMARY: The irrepressible Mem Fox shares her passionate and witty commentary on the power and importance of reading aloud, showing openly our love for books, writing with students, "burying" drafts that aren't working rather than making students tediously labor over them, and sharing books that do not try to "put a pretty face on real life" (p. 130). You will cheer Mem on as she shares her own fears and frustrations and raves with unbridled honesty about basal readers: "Children exposed only to basal readers must wonder why they should bother to learn to read when what they read provides so little pleasure or fascination" (p. 121). You will gain many insights about the reading-writing connection, and you will *never* be bored—you won't even look up after page 1.

Frank, Marjorie. *If You're Trying to Teach Kids How to Write . . . you've gotta have this book! 2nd edition.* **1995. Nashville: Incentive Publications, Inc. ISBN: 0-86530-317-7.**

SUMMARY: Practicality is Marjorie Frank's middle name. This book, a visual feast, packed to the brim with teaching ideas, is highly complementary to the six-trait method of instruction and assessment. It touches on virtually every trait, and each stage of the writing process as well. Frank also tunes in to teachers' worries: e.g., *What do I do when I run out of teaching ideas? How do I motivate students who don't want to write? Do I have to use portfolios? How do I make students less dependent on me?* All the while, Frank fills our heads with specific strategies and lesson ideas—not to mention suggested prompts (one of the *very few* authors to include these). Frank LOVES to teach writing, and it shows on every page. Cleverly illustrated, easy to convert into lessons, not overwhelmingly long. Ideal for K–8.

Gerson, Sharon J. and Steven M. Gerson. *Technical Writing: Process and Product, 3rd edition.* **1999. Upper Saddle River, NJ: Prentice Hall.** ISBN: **0-13-020871-X.**

SUMMARY: If you want it *all* between two covers—the be-all and end-all of tech writing—this is your book. It's thorough, readable, beautifully organized, and filled with numerous useful examples of everything from office memos to graphics to proposals. Nothing escapes Gerson and Gerson. Best of all, they take a writing process approach to the whole affair, treating tech writing as real-world writing, not something for technophiles only. Topics include working with computers, avoiding passive voice, being concise, organizing information, avoiding sexist language, designing your document so it achieves your objectives, and creating every kind of document from e-mail to reports, proposals, summaries, and oral presentations. A whole section is devoted to mechanics—and yes, tech editors *are* pickier (it's not just a rumor). Suggested lessons are included. Leans toward secondary, but adaptable to any grade level.

Gerson, Steven M. *Writing That Works.* **Kansas Competency Based Curriculum Center.**

SUMMARY: If you'd like a shorter, condensed version of the "whole works" book just listed, here it is. In this concise edition, Dr. Gerson actually puts the fun back into tech writing (even if you did not know it was ever there). He begins by teaching us the all-important lesson that in its broadest sense, "tech" writing includes the everyday writing so many of our students will be required to do in the workplace: memos, e-mails, reports, proposals, newsletters, instructions, resumes, web pages, etc. He then walks us through some innovative ways to weave such pieces into the curriculum without creating drudgery for student or teacher. The book is *packed* with teaching ideas—and excellent illustrations that will help you create your own lessons. It's concise, readable, very well laid-out, and a flat-out delight to read. Spans many grade levels, from elementary through high school and beyond.

Goldberg, Bonni. *Room to Write: Daily Invitations to a Writer's Life.* **1996. New York: G.P. Putnam's Sons.** ISBN: **0-87477-825-5.**

SUMMARY: Witty and wise, this book will bring out the talent in even the most reluctant writer. Goldberg's invitations to write range from practical to whimsical, but definitely lean toward the creative side. Each lesson includes an overview and tips on seeing the world through a writer's eyes, accompanied by an intriguing writing path to follow and provocative quotations from famous writers. Excellent for self-study or for classroom use.

Gordon, Karen Elizabeth. *The Deluxe Transitive Vampire: The Ultimate Handbook of Grammar for the Innocent, the Eager, and the Doomed.* **1993. New York: Random House.** ISBN: **0-679-41860-1.**

SUMMARY: How keen is *your* sense of grammar? "An assortment of odd chocolates and soft toffees *was/were* congealed in her alligator shoes." If you said *was,* your ear and knowledge of grammar did not betray you. This is but one of numerous intriguing, imaginative examples reflecting the best teaching on grammar around. Gordon makes this potentially dry subject fun, *engaging,* and *very* understandable. Want a little brush-up, or just a good book for regular reference that won't bore you to tears? Here it is. William Safire calls it "A book to sink your fangs into." You'll need to be selective in sharing with students; many of the illustrations are exceptionally—um—attention-getting.

Graves, Donald H. *A Fresh Look at Writing.* **1994. Portsmouth, NH: Heinemann.** ISBN: **0-435-088246.**

SUMMARY: This is Donald Graves' most outspoken—and therefore best—book. For example, when asked what to do if you can only teach writing once a week, Graves now tells teachers, "Don't teach it at all" since you can only teach poor writing habits within that time. That's a bold and honest answer and I like Graves a lot for saying it. Graves offers thorough discussions of revision, helping students share their writing, teaching conventions, and keeping your own expectations high. It's voicy and personal, a chat with the guru, and filled with good student examples.

Harvey, Stephanie. *Nonfiction Matters: Reading, Writing, and Research in Grades 3–8.* **1998. York, ME: Stenhouse Publishers.** ISBN: **1-57110-072-5.**

SUMMARY: This practical, down-to-earth book helps open doors to truly good nonfiction writing in 3–8 classrooms. Harvey begins at the beginning, with tips on finding good sources, taking notes, thinking through organization, and reading and using nonfiction. She takes us right through the process, showing numerous excellent examples along the way. You'll appreciate the emphasis she places on appropriate voice in nonfiction: the creation of accessible text. Especially useful are the thorough bibliographies included in the appendix.

Johnson, Bea. *Never Too Early to Write: Adventures in the K–1 Writing Workshop.* 1999. Gainesville, FL: Maupin House Publishing. ISBN: 0-929895-31-2.

SUMMARY: The very best book around for working with K–2 students. It's a small book, easy to pick up, quick to read. The focus is on the practical. Every page is jam-packed with ideas for teaching; illustrations abound. Johnson talks about setting up a writing center, integrating drawing and writing, teaching editing to young children, modeling, holding conferences—and virtually everything else you wish she would discuss. The text is written in user-friendly language, just as if she were having a chat with you. It's unpretentious and flat out wonderful. She calls it K–1, but since many of her illustrations (and ideas) apply to grades 2 and even 3, I encourage teachers at those levels to have a look also.

Johnson, Eric. *You Are the Editor: Sixty-One Editing Lessons that Improve Writing Skills.* 1981. Parsippany, NJ: Fearon Teacher Aids. ISBN: 0-8224-7696-7.

SUMMARY: One of the best books around on teaching editing *step by step*. Students learn copy editor's symbols, and how to apply them—one by one. That's the secret. They're never overwhelmed, and they become sharp editors through systematic, carefully designed practice. Lessons are *just* long enough, and answers are in the back, so you don't have to guess. Non-copyrighted blackline masters make this a book you can share. Ideal for grades 5 through 12. You can also use it with grades 3 and 4, though; just adapt and simplify a little. Shorten the lessons; take a couple errors out by retyping a paragraph or two. Use it daily if you can, but no less than twice per week.

Keene, Ellin Oliver and Susan Zimmermann. *Mosaic of Thought: Teaching Comprehension in a Reader's Workshop.* 1997. Portsmouth, NH: Heinemann. ISBN: 0-435-07237-4.

SUMMARY: How do students make sense of written text? What is the importance of reading in an interactive fashion, learning to pose questions, making inferences, synthesizing information, solving readers' problems and creating a "mosaic of thought" that interweaves personal experience with the written text of others? This book is an enlightening journey into how readers, especially *successful* readers, think. It is also a kind of workshop in itself that helps show teachers the how-to of good reading instruction. The link to writing? Keene and Zimmermann never miss an opportunity to make that crystal clear, but it is worth adding that students who understand how to read text with thought and insight are far more prepared to read their own writing in the same way, and hence to self-assess and revise.

Lamott, Anne. *Bird By Bird: Some Instructions on Writing and Life.* 1994. New York: Doubleday. ISBN: 0-385-48001-6.

SUMMARY: Anne Lamott does not try to make writing sound easy—as if all you need is some magic formula (or even more annoying) the right frame of mind, and presto, the words will flow. She recognizes that writing isn't always terrible, either; it's more often mediocre, which can leave you with the feeling that perhaps you *yourself* are mediocre, a depressing feeling with which to be left. This really isn't a book of lessons. You won't get 18 ideas for things you could do, as with Barry Lane or Donald Murray. This is more a book of comfort and philosophical truth. For example, Lamott tells us that to find [our] own true voice, [we] must "go through the one door in the castle that [we] have been told not to go through." We must "turn the unspeakable into words. Not just into any words but if (we) can, into rhythm and blues."

Lane, Barry. *After THE END: Teaching and Learning Creative Revision.* 1992. Portsmouth, NH: Heinemann. ISBN: 0-435-08714-2.

SUMMARY: A classic. Lane writes with such ease and grace that his books are pure joy to read. Not only is he blessed with a true comic voice, but he thinks of interesting, out-of-the-ordinary things to teach us about writing: turning questions into leads, exploding a moment or shrinking a century, and moving in close with your "binoculars,"—simple but ingenious writers' tricks that make writing both easier and more fun. Way back in eighth grade, Mrs. Lowery nearly died trying to teach us what a dangling participle was (a couple of us even got it), but knowing this won't make your writing all *that* much better. In contrast, knowing how to graph the high points of a story *will*. This book rings with the authenticity of someone who has actually been both writer and teacher, and knows how to combine them well.

Lane, Barry. *The Reviser's Toolbox.* 1998. Shoreham, VT: Discover Writing Press. ISBN: 0-965-65744-2.

VIC'S PICKS **SUMMARY:** Based on Lane's enormously popular seminars on revision, this wonderfully idea-rich text will help you guide young writers painlessly through the revision process. You'll have a wonderful time adapting Lane's highly creative lessons to fit your own style; your students will have an even better time working on writing activities that are both enjoyable and educational. This book is FULL of practical ideas you can use <u>right now</u> to make the concept of revision clear, and to help students expand detail, restructure information,become better critics, and work effectively both on their own and in response groups. Practical, entertaining, and easy to follow.

Lane, Barry and Andrew Green. *The Portfolio Source Book.* **1994. Shoreham, VT: Discover Writing Press.** ISBN: **0-965-65741-8.**

SUMMARY: Portfolios provide a richer picture of student writing performance than we can gain through any other method, and creating portfolios is an invaluable experience for students; yet many teachers have found them perplexing and even overwhelming. Through this book, you'll learn how to make portfolios manageable, and why you should bother trying. The students whose work is represented here make their own choices about what goes into the portfolio. As they do so, they learn about themselves as writers, assessing their growth, and discovering thereby who they are becoming as writers. Lane and Green show step by step how to turn the management of portfolios over to students so that the process becomes a learning experience, rather than an organizational nightmare for the teacher.

Lederer, Richard and Richard Dowis. *The Write Way.* **1995. New York: Simon and Schuster.** ISBN: **0-671-52670-7.**

SUMMARY: Richard Lederer is a stand-up comic who just happens also to be a linguist and a crackerjack writing teacher. The purpose of this book is to help readers master the 5 c's of good writing: *clear, correct, concise, complete, considerate.* In presenting this important information, Lederer and Dowis clearly and humorously teach such topics as cutting deadwood from writing, targeting writing to a specific audience, and avoiding common errors in syntax and grammar. Regular self-tests add to the fun and let you find out periodically if you're as good a writer, speller, or grammarian as you thought.

Mandelbaum, Paul, ed. *First Words: Earliest Writings from Favorite Contemporary Authors.* **1993. New York: Workman Publishing.** ISBN: **0-945575-71-8.**

SUMMARY: Ever wonder what the childhood writings of now-famous authors might have looked like? Or how you might have assessed them or responded had they been *your* students—just kids, yet unknown? Would you have recognized their potential? Find out as you explore the world of childhood writing with examples from Margaret Atwood, William S. Burroughs, Pat Conroy, Michael Crichton, Rita Dove, Amy Tan, Stephen King, Ursula K. Le Guin, and many others. The book, almost 500 pages long, includes photographs, some revision samples, anecdotes about the authors, and marginal notes to help make connections to earlier works.

Murray, Donald M. *Write to Learn*. 1984. New York: Holt, Rinehart and Winston. ISBN: 0-03-061996-3.

SUMMARY: This book takes us deep within the writing process, well beneath all that surface lock-step mechanics of webbing, then drafting, revising, sharing—as if writing were cookie baking. Murray recognizes that some people aren't making cookies. They're making Caesar salad, or quilts, or Oriental gardens. Murray also freely admits that this book will not teach you to write; it will simply help you teach *yourself* to write. That kind of honesty will win your heart every time. Go behind the scenes with Murray to see how the terrific story of his grandmother came together. His tips on writing well *will* help you.

Murray, Donald M. *A Writer Teaches Writing*. 2nd edition. 1985. New York: Houghton Mifflin. ISBN: 0-395-35441-2.

SUMMARY: Perhaps no one has a deeper understanding of the writing process than Donald Murray, or writes more eloquently about it, both from the perspective of a teacher and from that of a writer. You can read this book like a novel; it's that good. He speaks right to you, and he knows what you need to know to teach well. The book is filled with useful sections on writing good leads and endings, getting rid of filler, organizing information, building fluent sentences (Murray was already working with the traits, you see, *long* before we were), the writer as reader, and helping students work in groups. When Murray gets going on voice, he just *sings:* "Voice," claims Murray, "separates writing that is read from writing that is not read." Still the unsurpassed definition.

O'Conner, Patricia T. *Woe Is I: The Grammarphobe's Guide to Better English in Plain English*. 1996. New York: Putnam. ISBN: 0-399-14196-0.

SUMMARY: Don't know a "gerund from a gerbil"? Spend a few minutes (or longer—you won't want to stop) testing your knowledge of current grammatical correctness with a book that is the very most fun you can have with conventions. Reduce your fear of *lie/lay* choices. Learn whether to say, *"I use to love assessment"* or *"I used to love assessment."* Find out if *leapt, learnt* and *smelt* are real past tense verbs, or just oldies no one uses. What about *"I have just woken up?"* Can you talk like that? The coolest little book on grammar since Strunk and White. Just as punchy. Twice as funny. Get one for yourself; then quiz your students. Let them borrow the book and quiz you. Think you know your stuff? Find out.

O'Conner, Patricia T. *Words Fail Me: What Everyone Who Writes Should Know About Writing.* 1999. New York: Harcourt Brace & Company. ISBN: 0-15-100371-8.

SUMMARY: Here is the much-awaited sequel to *Woe Is I*, the very most fun anyone can have with conventions. In this highly witty resource, O'Connor explores such timely issues as connecting with your audience, getting rid of the baloney in your writing (don't say *eggplant* when you mean *purple*), depending on verbs, learning not to drown yourself (or your reader victim) in modifiers, thinking in paragraphs, making sure your writing makes sense, putting some backbone into your prose ("When you have something to say, look the reader in the eye and say it"), and writing with honesty and voice. Excellent advice, presented in O'Connor's inimitable style, with plenty of wit, liveliness, and wisdom. It's short. You can read it in an evening. Countless passages are quotable and sharable with students. It will make you a finer writer and teacher of writing.

Palmer, Parker J. *The Courage to Teach: Exploring the Inner Landscape of a Teacher's Life.* 1998. San Francisco: Jossey-Bass Publishers. ISBN: 0-7879-1058-9.

SUMMARY: A philosophical journey that takes you deep within your own mind and heart. This book is based on the premise that how we teach and how *well* we teach depends much less upon technique and strategy than upon who we are, and on how we connect ourselves, our subjects and our students into one intricate fabric of learning. It will touch you, and take you back to the ideals and hopes that first made you want to teach. Insightful and deeply satisfying.

Romano, Tom. *Writing With Passion.* 1995. Portsmouth, NH: Greenwood-Heinemann. ISBN: 0-86709-362-5.

SUMMARY: Romano is so unflinchingly honest and writes, as his title suggests, with such passion, it must be an exhilarating experience to be among his students. He holds student work in high esteem, and the book is filled with telling examples, both from their work and from Romano's own. He speaks honestly about the need for courage in writing, and our obligation to create an environment in which courage is rewarded. Wonderful discussions of research, poetry, grading, and many other timely topics. Of special interest are sections on multiple genre writing, which Romano handles with zest and insight.

Routman, Regie. *Conversations: Strategies for Teaching, Learning, and Evaluating.* 1999. Portsmouth, NH: Heinemann. ISBN: 0-325-00109-X.

SUMMARY: An incredibly comprehensive, highly readable text that covers virtually every phase of teaching reading and writing, with numerous anecdotes and samples to lend authenticity. Routman is knowledgeable, experienced, and very down to earth; she is not afraid to admit she has changed her mind about a few once-beloved strategies that didn't work! Here is plain talk on teaching well: a wealth of it. The text is vast, and expansively addresses such issues as organizing the classroom for writing, setting appropriate expectations (we tend to aim too low or too high, Routman cautions), sharing your own writing with students, sharing nonfiction, holding conferences, encouraging reflection, teaching revision and editing, fostering independent reading, literature response, and oh so much more. A huge book worth the effort it takes to hoist it off the shelf.

Sebranek, Patrick, et al. *Write Source*® **Handbooks for Students. (Dated individually.) Wilmington, MA: Great Source Education Group, Inc.**

SUMMARY: This remarkable collection comprises the most student-friendly texts anywhere on the planet. Students are enthralled with the pictures, and engaged by text that is written right *to* them, not around them or for them or about them. Every line is understandable, so they *get* it. As a teacher, you can make use of an accompanying Program Guide, so easy to follow, so rich with blackline master ready-to-go lessons, you'll wonder how you taught writing without it. If it has to do with writing—process, traits, modes and genres, research, examples, finding a topic, methods and strategies, work place writing, revision and editing, writing citations correctly, prewriting to publishing—you will find it in these impressive, welcoming books. Best of all, the handbooks are grade level specific, so one size need *not* fit all. Tailor-made to help your students become the best writers they can be, without the pain. Well, *mostly* without the pain. They *do* still need to write (not even these authors could find a way around that one).

- Grade 1   *Write ONE*   ISBN: 0-669-45975-5
- Grade 2   *Write Away*   ISBN :0-669-48234-X
- Grade 3   *Write on Track*   ISBN: 0-669-48220-X
- Grades 4–5 *Writers Express*   ISBN: 0-669-47163-1
- Grades 6–8 *Write Source 2000*   ISBN: 0-669-46773-1
- High School *Writers INC*   ISBN: 0-669-47164-X
- High School *School to Work*   ISBN: 0-669-40874-3
- High School/College *Write for College*   ISBN: 0-669-44401-4

Spandel, Vicki and Richard J. Stiggins. *Creating Writers.*
2nd edition. 1996. New York: Addison Wesley Longman.
ISBN: 0-8013-1578-6.

SUMMARY: What students can assess, they can revise; that's the theme of a book that will help you assess consistently and, more important, use assessment as a foundation for powerful writing instruction. Through this revised edition (with even more emphasis on using the 6-trait model in the classroom), you'll discover that assessment isn't really about whipping up mounds of data; it's about getting inside writing (or any content area) to figure out the difference between the good and the not-so-good. Students who can do that can revise; self-assessment puts them in charge of their own writing process and sets them on the path to lifelong learning. The most complete book available on 6-trait writing and assessment, beautifully compatible with all *Write Source* handbooks for students (See Sebranek, et al. the *Write Source* handbooks for students, this section).

Steele, Bob. *Draw Me a Story: An Illustrated Exploration of Drawing as Language.* **1998. Winnipeg, Canada: Penguin Publishers.**
ISBN: 1-895411-82-3.

SUMMARY: We have long contended that in young children, both ideas and voice—even fluency—reveal themselves first in art, then in text. This idea is richly, beautifully confirmed in this marvelous exploration of art, primarily from very young children, but from some more sophisticated student artists as well. In this book, language is defined as "any symbolic system, coded or uncoded, which facilitates articulation, expression, and communication of perceptions, thoughts, and feelings" (p. 17). A deep, probing look at the evolution of children's drawings, the developmental thinking that accompanies it, and the many ways drawing can be used to help children build observation skills, solve problems, express inner emotions, celebrate friendship or community, *and* tell stories.

Stevens, Carla. *A Book of Your Own: Keeping a Diary or Journal.*
1993. New York: Houghton Mifflin Company. ISBN: 0-89919-256-4.

SUMMARY: Students often have difficulty knowing what to write in a journal, or thinking of *anything* to say at all. Here's a book you can use to diminish the horror of the blank page. It includes not only tips on making journal writing more fun (including toting your journal with you), but also samples from actual journals, some from students, some from known writers, including Anne Frank, Beatrix Potter, Teddy Roosevelt, Louisa May Alcott, and others. What did Teddy have to say on a dull day, anyhow? You will be surprised how inspired your journal writers may be when they hear the entries of others, some of them extremely simple. It's a book that let's us peek inside what is normally very private writing.

Stiggins, Richard J. *Student-Centered Classroom Assessment.* 2nd edition. 1996. Columbus, OH: Prentice Hall (Merrill). ISBN: 0-13-432931-7.

SUMMARY: Probably the most complete look at the world of quality assessment, and how to make assessment work for you and your students in the classroom. Stiggins invites you to think about such topics as choosing the right assessment method to fit your situation, communicating with various audiences about student achievement, keeping assessment targets clear and ensuring that they're important, overcoming barriers to quality assessment, understanding and using essay assessment and performance assessment, finding the proper role for portfolios within the classroom, gaining perspective on standardized testing, and much, much more. Provocative questions at the end of each chapter and suggested activities offer opportunities for extending learning, especially in a group context.

Strickland, Kathleen and James. *Reflections on Assessment: Its Purposes, Methods, and Effects on Learning.* 1998. Portsmouth, NH: Greenwood-Heinemann. ISBN: 0-86709-445-1.

SUMMARY: An eyes-wide-open overview of today's assessment world, filled with anecdotes of real-life teachers coping with a wide range of testing situations. Their stories are used purposefully, to make important points about testing and its impact on our curriculum and our society. Deeply influenced by the philosophies of Donald Murray and Grant Wiggins, this is a rich and thorough book, a mini-course in assessment, with special attention given to such timely subjects as standards, rubric development and use, kinds of assessment, the values (and pitfalls) of alternative assessment, student involvement in assessment, standardized tests (their use and misuse), grading, communication with parents and school boards, and much, much more. The whole book is written in a friendly, conversational style that truly does invite us to reflect on testing issues and on the role every educator plays in upholding traditions and/or introducing testing innovations: "We are the professionals, and we are responsible for making this happen—for all kids, in all schools." (p. 211)

Thomason, Tommy. *Writer to Writer: How to Conference Young Authors.* **1998. Norwood, MA: Christopher Gordon Publishers.** ISBN: **0-926842-79-X.**

SUMMARY: Don't you find that the older you get, the more you love skinny books? Not to mention short chapters, practical advice, less theory—and more substance. If you'd like to learn the in's and out's of student conferences, K–8, from turning a conference into a conversation to helping young writers conference each other, this is your book. It's eminently practical, and rings with authenticity. Tommy is a master at taking something complex and keeping it simple and manageable. If you've read Graves, Calkins, and Murray and you're *still* not sure what to do, try Tommy's book. He turns the light on.

Thomason, Tommy and Carol York. *Write on Target: Preparing Young Writers to Succeed on State Writing Achievement Tests.* **2000. Norwood, MA: Christopher Gordon Publishers.** ISBN: **0-926842-98-6.**

SUMMARY: Just as skinny as Tommy's other books, and just as filled with substance. This is not a philosophical discussion on whether we should have writing assessments, or whether we should reform them; it takes the position that they're *here*—at least for now—so we must help our students turn in their best performances. How do we do that? Thomason and York emphasize the use of rubrics in teaching, demonstrating differences among forms (e.g., narrative vs. expository), modeling writing for students, and sharing literature. Their tips are practical, to the point, and designed to build student confidence.

The University of Chicago Press. *The Chicago Manual of Style: The Essential Guide for Writers, Editors, and Publishers.* **14th edition. 1993. Chicago: University of Chicago Press.** ISBN: **0-226-10389-7.**

SUMMARY: Chicago has given the world so much more than great sports teams, fabulous steaks, world-class theater, and great memories of Siskel & Ebert. There's also the *Chicago Manual of Style*—emphasis on style, for this is a classy book. It's a summary of what the well-informed editor needs to know, presented clearly and in the most orderly fashion. It's strictly a reference book, though—no light reading here. You may not want to take it on an airplane, but *do* keep it at your desk. It's complete and thoughtfully organized, highly authoritative, and not voiceless, either, contrary to popular opinion.

Wilhelm, Jeffrey D. "You Gotta BE the Book.": Teaching Engaged and Reflective Reading with Adolescents. 1996. New York: Teachers College Press. ISBN: 0-8077-3566-3.

SUMMARY: A remarkable book on the nature of reading, and on ways to encourage literacy among young adolescents. Far from a quick-fix overview, this book represents a profound look into what successful readers do, and how to translate that into classroom practice. Of particular interest is Wilhelm's exploration of drama as a means of expanding and enriching a reader's response to a text. In addition, though, he looks at ways to engage students, including reluctant readers, and cheerfully but honestly offers a critique of things we do, often with the best of intentions, that discourage young readers, or even turn them into nonreaders. This book is written in such a teacher-friendly style, it's like sitting down with Jeff for a cup of coffee. (See also *Mosaic of Thought,* Ellin Oliver Keene and Susan Zimmermann, this section.)

Wooldridge, Susan Goldsmith. *poemcrazy: freeing your life with words.* 1996. New York: Random House. ISBN: 0-609-80098-1.

SUMMARY: Some might call this a book on writing poetry. Really, though, it's a book on writing your thoughts, feelings, imaginings, and possibilities in the *form* of poetry. It is full of whimsy and imagination, a book intended to teach us about the poetry that lives in us all and is embedded within our lives, if only we know how to look for it. Chapters are very short and organized to present a reflective piece first, then invite readers to participate in a relevant poetry writing activity. *Many* lesson ideas for those who already enjoy teaching poetry—and for those who thought they might if only they knew how to begin.

Zinsser, William. *On Writing Well: The Classic Guide to Writing Nonfiction. 6th edition.* 1998. New York: HarperCollins. ISBN: 0-06-273523-3.

SUMMARY: Zinsser's writing contains *no fluff.* It's all substance. You can turn to any page at random and come away with a jewel. Also, he isn't lofty or pedantic—ever. He doesn't need to be because his advice is so good he can express it in simple terms: "I wrote one book about baseball and one about jazz. But it never occurred to me to write one of them in sports English and the other in jazz English" (p. 234). It is hard to write profound thoughts in plain words. That's why Zinsser's books are models of the craft. Also, Zinsser knows what is *important* to teach: voice, substance, avoiding phoniness, knowing your topic, and turning nonfiction into literature. He also includes special sections on memoir, business writing, sports writing, science and technology, and writing a good critique.

Zinsser, William. *Writing to Learn.* 1988. New York: HarperCollins. ISBN: 0-06-272040-6.

SUMMARY: Zinsser claims to have written this book to "ease two fears that American education seems to inflict on all of us in some form." He refers to fear of writing, and fear of subjects we think we're not very good at: for some of us, these are the same thing. This book takes us into the world of writing to learn *and* to explain art, science, math, social science, or any topic. As always, Zinsser shows us the importance and the how-to of stripping language down to its basics, getting rid of pretentiousness, and writing clearly by thinking clearly. Essential for anyone who uses writing as a tool to help students think logically and organize their thoughts in a way that makes sense to others. Ideal for expository, research, business, and tech writing classes. Excellent examples, too.

Index of Books by Author and Title

Y

Z